Rescuing Ellisville Marsh

OTHER BOOKS FROM BRIGHT LEAF

House Stories: The Meanings of Home in a New England Town
BETH LUEY

Bricklayer Bill: The Untold Story of the Workingman's Boston Marathon
PATRICK L. KENNEDY AND LAWRENCE W. KENNEDY

*Concrete Changes: Architecture, Politics, and
the Design of Boston City Hall*
BRIAN M. SIRMAN

Williamstown and Williams College: Explorations in Local History
DUSTIN GRIFFIN

Massachusetts Treasures: A Guide to Marvelous, Must-See Museums
CHUCK D'IMPERIO

*Boston's Twentieth-Century Bicycling Renaissance: Cultural Change on Two
Wheels*
LORENZ J. FINISON

Went to the Devil: A Yankee Whaler in the Slave Trade
ANTHONY J. CONNORS

At Home: Historic Houses of Eastern Massachusetts
BETH LUEY

*Black Lives, Native Lands, White Worlds: A History of Slavery in
New England*
JARED ROSS HARDESTY

At Home: Historic Houses of Central and Western Massachusetts
BETH LUEY

Flight Calls: Exploring Massachusetts through Birds
JOHN R. NELSON

*Lost Wonderland: The Brief and Brilliant Life of
Boston's Million Dollar Amusement Park*
STEPHEN R. WILK

I Believe I'll Go Back Home: Roots and Revival in New England Folk Music
THOMAS S. CURREN

Legends of the Common Stream
JOHN HANSON MITCHELL

Mind and Hearts: The Story of James Otis Jr. and Mercy Otis Warren
JEFFREY H. HACKER

The Combat Zone: Murder, Race, and Boston's Struggle for Justice
JAN BROGAN

*Letters from Red Farm: The Untold Story of the Friendship between
Helen Keller and Journalist Joseph Edgar Chamberlin*
ELIZABETH EMERSON

A Union Like Ours: The Love Story of F. O. Matthiessen and Russell Cheney
SCOTT BANE

Trail Running Eastern Massachusetts
BEN KIMBALL

RESCUING ELLISVILLE MARSH

The Long Fight
to Restore
Lost Connections

Eric P. Cody

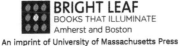
BRIGHT LEAF
BOOKS THAT ILLUMINATE
Amherst and Boston
An imprint of University of Massachusetts Press

Rescuing Ellisville Marsh has been supported by the Regional Books Fund, established by donors in 2019 to support the University of Massachusetts Press's Bright Leaf imprint.

Bright Leaf, an imprint of the University of Massachusetts Press, publishes accessible and entertaining books about New England. Highlighting the history, culture, diversity, and environment of the region, Bright Leaf offers readers the tools and inspiration to explore its landmarks and traditions, famous personalities, and distinctive flora and fauna.

ISBN 978-1-62534-677-3 (paper); 678-0 (hardcover)

Designed by Sally Nichols
Set in Minion Pro
Printed and bound by Books International, Inc.

Cover design by Sally Nichols
Cover photo by Karin Engstrom (deceased), *Mossing at Ellisville Marsh,* ca. 1960.
Courtesy of Kristina Engstrom.

Library of Congress Cataloging-in-Publication Data
Names: Cody, Eric P., 1950– author.
Title: Rescuing Ellisville marsh : the long fight to restore lost
connections / Eric P. Cody.
Description: Amherst : Bright Leaf, an imprint of University of
Massachusetts Press, [2023] | Includes bibliographical references and
index.
Identifiers: LCCN 2022022530 (print) | LCCN 2022022531 (ebook) | ISBN
9781625346773 (paperback) | ISBN 9781625346780 (hardcover) | ISBN
9781613769577 (ebook) | ISBN 9781613769584 (ebook)
Subjects: LCSH: Salt marsh conservation—Massachusetts—Plymouth. | Salt
marsh restoration—Massachusetts—Plymouth. | BISAC: HISTORY / United
States / State & Local / New England (CT, MA, ME, NH, RI, VT) | NATURE /
Environmental Conservation & Protection
Classification: LCC QH76.5.M4 C63 2023 (print) | LCC QH76.5.M4 (ebook) |
DDC 333.7209744/82—dc23/eng/20220831
LC record available at https://lccn.loc.gov/2022022530
LC ebook record available at https://lccn.loc.gov/2022022531

British Library Cataloguing-in-Publication Data
A catalog record for this book is available from the British Library.

"Never doubt that a small group of thought-
ful, committed citizens can change the world;
indeed, it's the only thing that ever has."

—Margaret Mead

Contents

Preface

IN JULY 2007, FIVE neighbors on Lookout Point in Plymouth, Massachusetts, formed a nonprofit called Friends of Ellisville Marsh, Inc., to solve an erosion problem. The unchecked migration of a nearby salt marsh inlet was threatening homes perched atop the coastal bank. Others soon joined the effort. Once the immediate problem had been addressed, the group's focus shifted to restoring tidal flows to the salt marsh for the revitalization of fisheries and wildlife.

Within a decade the project had garnered a wide community of support and marked its success in myriad ways. The group acquired all the necessary local, state, and federal permits to maintain the marsh inlet on a continuing basis and periodically reopened it after major storms. A treasure trove of scientific monitoring data was collected. A model for protecting nesting areas of threatened shorebirds created. A new species of insect discovered. A second nonprofit spun off. It all revolved around a prized natural resource.

This is the story of a special place whose roots are buried deeply in the sands of time. A story of monster storms, fishing weirs and lobster carrs, sea moss harvesting, invisible birds, tiny discoveries, wildlife rescues, wondrous migrations, and a constantly changing shoreline. A story about reaching into the past and delving deeply into the present to understand what defines a natural place, uncovering what truly matters, and learning how to live more closely with nature.

Front-line volunteers experienced the joys and tragedies of observing wildlife up close and personally, along with the frustrations of dealing with regulations and public agency officials often too far removed from the natural areas they control. This is a story of people who, like those preceding them, connected with a natural place and in the process learned something important about themselves.

My preoccupation with Ellisville Marsh began in late 2003, shortly after my wife Christine and I bought our home on Lookout Point in Plymouth, Massachusetts. From our tiny lawn atop the coastal bank, one can on a clear day see Provincetown's tall monument and water tank some twenty-five miles distant across Cape Cod Bay.

The ocean appears greenish gray, except on days when a bright sun is directly overhead. On these days, the water turns blue-green and one can discern the outline of the eelgrass bed ten feet below its surface. Just to the north are sand and cobble bars and an old rock jetty that sits just beyond the northern side of the Ellisville Marsh inlet and channel.

On a cold day late in November 2003, construction equipment was on the barrier beach working loudly to reopen the blocked salt marsh inlet. The project's purpose was to straighten the inlet, which had become so badly diverted that water spilling out of the marsh when the tide ebbed had to follow an elongated course to the bay. This made it impossible for the marsh to drain properly before the tide turned and the water began flooding back in.

The tidal channel had angled a quarter mile southward, putting pressure on the coastal bank and eroding the forty-foot bluff that ran along a neighbor's property. The neighbor had undertaken the inlet excavation project in his own self-interest and at his own expense. He was losing as much as fifteen feet every year, and if the channel diversion was not addressed, his cottage would eventually fall over the edge.

My clearest memory of that day was the gush of water erupting into the bay when the excavator finally broke through that last, thin remnant of the barrier spit that held back the pent-up water. The dam broke, releasing hundreds of thousands of gallons in a mad torrent. Its rip current churned up waves a quarter mile out in the bay. It was as though the seventy-acre salt marsh had exhaled deeply. I could almost hear the sigh of relief. I was enthralled. And so began an odyssey.

What began as an effort to save private property turned into a crusade to restore the vitality of fisheries and wildlife in a salt marsh. Many others joined the effort. The journey has been arduous. We opened a window into nature, and what we saw changed us.

Certain aspects of the telling of this story require explanation. Foremost, the opinions expressed in this book are mine and mine alone and are not intended to represent the views of any other individual, organization, or entity. Efforts have been made to ensure that statements made herein are scientifically correct. However, I am not a scientist, nor is this book intended to be a scientific reference. Instead, these observations reflect the experiences of a layperson who spent fifteen years closely observing a natural resource area and marveling at what he saw.

Acknowledgments

I EXPRESS MY SINCERE appreciation to the following individuals whose critical reviews and subject matter expertise helped to ensure that this book is factually correct and told in a way that makes its lessons accessible to the widest possible audience:

- Alan Cody
- David Gould
- Becky Harris
- Irina Kadis
- Paula Marcoux
- Ed Reiner
- Ellen Russell
- Peter Schwartzman

I also acknowledge all the individuals who have served with me on the board of directors of the Friends of Ellisville Marsh, Inc. The existence of this book demonstrates that what we have accomplished together is meaningful and consequential.

Finally, I dedicate this book to the late Albert Marsh, whose gift of land he loved was the foundation stone of an effort to revitalize and preserve the unique, natural heritage of Ellisville Marsh for future generations, and to Donald Quinn, who spent years tracking down the far-flung owners of fractionalized land parcels so that Ellisville Marsh in its entirety could be permanently protected. Without the efforts and sacrifices of these two individuals and their families, I would not be recounting this experience.

Main Characters

- Doug Johnson, a pulmonologist whose avocation is the eradication of Japanese knotweed
- Ed Reiner, a senior wetland scientist with the US Environmental Protection Agency
- John Ramsey, geo-coastal engineer with Applied Coastal Research and Engineering
- Bob Goldthwaite, a founding director of the Friends and former sea mosser
- Peter Hruby, a founding director of the Friends
- Paul Martino, former Ellisville resident and past president of the Lookout Point Improvement Association
- Bobbi Martino, a member of the threatened species monitoring team
- Paula Marcoux, a Friends director and member of the threatened species monitoring team
- Diane Jordan, a Friends director and member of the threatened species monitoring team
- Brad Winn, a former Friends director and vice president of Resilient Habitats at Manomet
- Kelley O'Neel, a former Friends director and member of the beach transect measurement team
- Frank Doyle, a Friends director
- Peter Schwartzman, a former Friends director and president of the Savery Pond Conservancy
- Henry Riter, a former Friends director
- Kim Tower, a former Friends director and environmental technician in Plymouth's Department of Marine and Environmental Affairs
- Mike Brennan, a pilot from Fairhaven, Massachusetts
- Sarah Cowles, the Friends' first environmental monitoring intern
- Chris Foley, an environmental monitoring intern
- Randy Parker, owner of the survey firm Land Management Systems, Inc.
- Stan Humphries, a former principal with LEC Environmental Consultants, Inc.
- Greg Lano, the Friends member who orchestrates meetings with elected state officials
- Brian Richmond, a local excavation contractor experienced in coastal work
- Jason Richmond and Brian Richmond Jr., excavation contractors
- Mary Ellen Mastrorilli, a member of the beach transect measurement team

- Ellen Jedrey, former assistant director of Mass Audubon's Coastal Waterbird Program
- Christine Cody, a member of the threatened species monitoring team
- Rosemary Smith, a member of the threatened species monitoring team
- Erik Boyer, stewardship manager at the Wildlands Trust
- Leah and Brad Bares, former Friends members
- Veda, the Bares's Newfoundland dog
- Judy Quinn, a Friends member
- Baker family, Friends members

PROJECT PARTNERS

- Coastal Waterbird Program of Mass Audubon (https://www.mas-saudubon.org/our-conservation-work/wildlife-research-conserva-tion/coastal-waterbird-program)
- Friends of Ellisville Marsh, Inc. (https://ellisvillemarsh.org)
- Salicicola.com (http://www.salicicola.com/checklists/Ellisville/)
- Savery Pond Conservancy (https://www.saverypond.org)
- Town of Plymouth (https://www.plymouth-ma.gov)
- Wildlands Trust (https://wildlandstrust.org)

PUBLIC AGENCIES WITH PERMIT-GRANTING AUTHORITY:

- MA Department of Environmental Protection (MassDEP)
- MA Environmental Policy Act Office (MEPA)
- Plymouth Conservation Commission (ConCom)
- US Army Corps of Engineers (USACE)

PUBLIC AGENCIES WITH AN ADVISORY ROLE IN PERMITTING:

- MA Areas of Critical Environmental Concern Program (ACEC)
- MA Division of Conservation and Recreation (DCR)
- MA Division of Marine Fisheries (DMF)
- MA Natural Heritage and Endangered Species Program (NHESP)
- MA Office of Coastal Zone Management (CZM)
- US Environmental Protection Agency (USEPA)
- US Fish and Wildlife Service (USFWS)

Chronology

CA. 11,000 BC	Paleoindians migrate to New England from other parts of North America.
1616–18	Wampanoag tribe flees "the plague" in other South Shore areas and encamps in Ellisville.
1620	The *Mayflower* lands and Pilgrims establish what will become the Massachusetts Bay Colony.
1857	Henry David Thoreau stops overnight at Ellis's Tavern and records his observations.
1890–1920	Fishing weir is operated at the Ellisville Marsh inlet.
1898	The Portland Gale moves the Ellisville Marsh inlet to its current-day location.
1960	The Commonwealth of Massachusetts constructs a rock jetty on the north side of the Ellisville Marsh inlet.
1978	The Great Blizzard of '78 hammers the Massachusetts coastline.
1982	The Commonwealth of Massachusetts designates Ellisville Harbor as an Area of Critical Environmental Concern (ACEC).
1986	Albert Marsh, one of the last lobstermen to work out of Ellisville Harbor, removes his boat after being sued by the Commonwealth. Maintenance of the Ellisville Marsh inlet is discontinued.
1991	Hurricane Bob blocks the tidal inlet. A few months later, the Perfect Storm, also called the No-Name Storm, smashes into the Massachusetts coastline.
	Ellisville Harbor State Park is created. It includes the northern half of the salt marsh.

1993
The Storm of the Century paralyzes Massachusetts.

2002
Vlad Hruby requests emergency authorization from the MassDEP and other agencies to reopen the blocked inlet to alleviate erosion of the coastal bank on which his home sits.

2003
Shifting Lots Preserve is created on property gifted to the Wildlands Trust by several local families. The new preserve includes the southern half of the salt marsh.

Ellisville Harbor is designated an Important Bird Area by Mass Audubon.

The blocked Ellisville Marsh inlet is reopened for the first time in nearly twenty years by Hruby.

2006
The MassDEP brings an enforcement action against Hruby for unauthorized work on the Ellisville Marsh inlet.

2007
Friends of Ellisville Marsh, Inc., is formed.

2008
The Friends submit initial project request under the Massachusetts Environmental Policy Act.

2010
A new species of insect is discovered in Ellisville Marsh by Ellen Russell and colleagues at the University of Massachusetts–Amherst

Last of the required permits for maintenance of the Ellisville Marsh inlet is issued to the Friends.

2011
The Friends reopen the blocked inlet for the first time since 2003.

2012
Superstorm Sandy hits Massachusetts.

The Election Day Storm hits Massachusetts.

2013
The Blizzard of 2013 (Winter Storm Nemo) hits Massachusetts.

2017
Project to develop a sustainable, long-term solution at Ellisville Marsh inlet kicks off.

2018
The Blizzard of 2018, a.k.a, the Bomb Cyclone Blizzard, hits Massachusetts.

2020
Albert Marsh dies.

Rescuing Ellisville Marsh

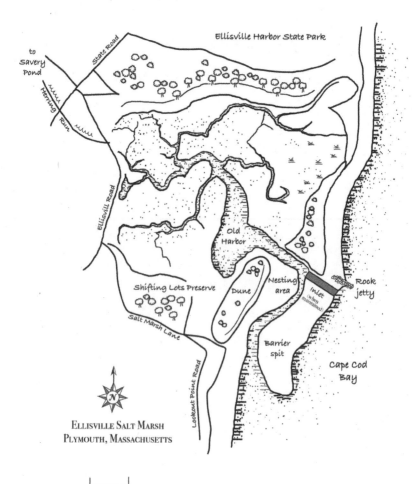

Ellisville Harbor State Park

to Savery Pond

State Road

Herring River

Ellisvill Road

Old Harbor

Shifting Lots Preserve

Salt Marsh Lane

Dune

Nesting area

Inlet (when maintained)

Rook jetty

Barrier spit

Cape Cod Bay

Lookout Point Road

N

Ellisville Salt Marsh
Plymouth, Massachusetts

500 feet

Graphic by Ann Marie Cody

CHAPTER 1

A Place Called Ellisville Marsh

WE HAVE STRANDED THE natural places. Broken their bonds with nature. Made them islands in a rising sea called *the built environment*. We have subdivided, excavated, erected, planted, and landscaped to create our own naturalistic domains. We see ourselves as landscape painters granted artistic license, beguile ourselves into believing we can portray nature, improve on what is already there with a few brushstrokes. Some think we have tamed nature or paid homage with our parks and gardens. But all we have done is cut up nature into smaller and smaller wild pieces.

A labyrinth of rules governs the leftover wilds. Navigating these rules to save what remains requires perseverance. The rules, and those who apply them, are not always well informed. They fail to see the interconnectedness of natural systems fractured by streets, highways, shopping malls, and power lines. Wildlife corridors and migration paths are severed by our never-ending propensity to build. Rivers, streams, and channels are choked. Salt marshes are dying.

Natural places are shown on maps as attractions worth visiting, small patches here and there shaded green. But visits are not enough. Natural places plead with us to be observed, experienced, appreciated, and valued for the windows into the wild they represent—for the peace and solitude they bring us, for the intimate, soul-touching connections they offer. They beg us to enter unreservedly and to breathe deeply, to listen for natural harmonies, to allow the setting to envelop us as though we were actors entering a scene. Walking, paddling, swimming, or bird watching in a natural place delivers more than appreciation. Just being present can engender feelings of reverence. Ellisville Marsh is such a place.

To float into Ellisville Marsh on the incoming tide is to enter another world. Drifting with the currents, paddling softly through the narrow channels, feeling the southwesterly breeze touch your skin after it has bent the tall shafts of saltmarsh cordgrass, is to escape all that is unimportant and insignificant. To experience this place closely is to be, in an instant, transfixed by its beauty and awed by its complexity. Here is the essence of nature, and in its embrace we find keys to our beginning and our survival. Ellisville Marsh is the environmental gem of New England's oldest town.

A Town Defined by Water

Plymouth, Massachusetts, proclaims itself to be "America's Hometown." The claim is irrefutable. It even says so on license plates. This seaside town descends over four hundred years from New England's first European settlement. It is also, by its hundred-square-mile-plus land area, the largest municipality in the Commonwealth of Massachusetts.

Plymouth may at first glance seem to be a rough-and-tumble place where people show small regard for the environment. Legions of motorcycles arrive on summer weekends with almost military precision, their smoke and thunder carrying up the streets that connect the waterfront with the center of town and Burial Hill. Lobster boats power by kayakers and sailboats in the harbor with reckless abandon, their radiating wakes rocking the smaller boats violently from side to side. Four-wheel-drive vehicles assert themselves on ocean beaches, with some drivers openly expressing disdain for rules that protect nesting shore-birds. Plastic liquor nip bottles cast from car windows dot the verges of rural roads. But do not be misled. Underneath all this is a town blessed with an incredible natural setting and people who care deeply about preserving it.

Plymouth is a place defined by water. Its 450 ponds and 36 miles of coastline are prized natural resources. Water is the engine that drives the local economy—and everything else. Seawater and freshwater run together in the town's veins. The steady pulse of the tides is Plymouth's heartbeat.

People who fish ply the ocean and ponds here. Everyone has a boat or knows someone who does. This community lives by the water and on the water. Its survival has for generations depended on inhabitants' abilities to live in close harmony with the sea, from Indigenous people who arrived thirteen thousand years ago to current-day residents. It is vital to draw lessons from this ages-old experience as the sea alters its relationship with us in ways our forebearers could not have imagined. Nor could any have foreseen that we would be the ones to precipitate a change in the fundamental rhythm of the sea.

Miles of open space and protected lands afford Plymouth residents and visitors a breathtaking range of opportunities to experience nature. There are coastal beaches, freshwater ponds, oak forests, and one of the largest remaining pine barrens in the world.[1] But there is a downside to all this natural bounty. Plymouth's vast expanse makes land more affordable than in neighboring towns within commuting range of Boston, so housing development is unrelentingly and unrepentantly robust.

The Pinehills, a mixed-use development set in 10,000 acres of scrub pine forest, will by the time it is complete have added some 3,000 new homes to the mix. It is not the only source of growth. The number of homes in town increased by more than 20 percent between 2000 and 2016, a gain of some 4,500 housing units. This reflects the recent trend. Half the housing units in Plymouth were built within the last fifty years. The other half took three hundred and fifty.

New homes are materializing everywhere. The most

sought-after sites are on the water—oceanfront and edge of pond. Hillside settings with even distant water views are also in high demand. Trees that get in the way of the view are unceremoniously cut down. Postage stamp–size lots that sat empty for decades are being built on. The sounds of chain saws and construction equipment can be heard across town. At times they seem to call to one another as though some new, invasive species has bullied its way into the ecosystem. The machines are symptomatic of an ongoing threat to nature in America's hometown. Housing development is running rampant, and natural resources are being sacrificed to make room for more people.

A contest is being waged over land. Developers are intent on acquiring some of the largest remaining tracts of undisturbed land in eastern Massachusetts, driven by their confidence that new homes in a pristine, naturalistic setting within reach of Boston will be highly marketable. Competing with them are nonprofits and town committees tasked with identifying and acquiring properties with intrinsic natural value for permanent protection. It is a race against time. For the developers the payoff is short-term return on investment. For the locals the benefits are timeless and priceless, a legacy of natural treasures to be passed on to children and grandchildren.

Plymouth is not a wealthy town, at least not in comparison with its better-dressed South Shore neighbors—Duxbury, Cohasset, and Hingham among them. But the town has visionaries determined to make their town a place where future generations will want to live because of its many connections to nature. A handful of citizens have made outsized contributions in educating their Plymouth neighbors about natural resources and championing environmental restoration projects.

Former Planning Board chair Malcolm MacGregor is one of these people. He has worked tirelessly for years to promote the concept of an "emerald necklace" of natural spaces and hiking paths that will encircle the town and connect to the sea at its northern and southern ends. He is known beyond his town committee role, having served on the faculty of the Massachusetts Maritime Academy for nearly fifty years.

MacGregor can often be encountered leading backwoods hikes in largely untraveled areas around town. Old Indian trails, cart paths, and dirt tracks are everywhere. He seems to have found them all. He is at ease being called "Trail Guy" in spite of his more distinguished titles of "professor" or "Planning Board chair." MacGregor is always approachable. He relishes questions about Plymouth trails and anything else related to the town's natural setting.

The town itself has shone a bright light on its natural resources by undertaking a series of wetlands restoration projects over the past twenty years. These projects have helped expand Plymouth's draw beyond its well-known historical sites: Plymouth Rock, the *Mayflower II* replica ship, the Plimoth Patuxet reproduction seventeenth-century village (formerly known as Plimoth Plantation), all of which have long been featured in tourist guides.

One initiative by the town's Department of Marine and Environmental Affairs, led by an unassuming yet remarkable environmental leader named David Gould, restored Town Brook. Centuries-old dams were lowered or removed in a sixteen-year series of projects to restore this herring run that connects Billington Sea, the headwaters of Town Brook, with Cape Cod Bay. In recognition of this and other wetlands restoration projects Plymouth was designated as the North American headquarters for World Fish Migration Day in 2020.

The Eel River Headwaters Restoration, another Town project, restored forty acres of decommissioned cranberry bogs and nearly two miles of streambed to their long-ago, natural state. This project included the planting of more than seventeen thousand Atlantic white cedar trees, among other back-to-nature interventions.

Environmental restoration projects undertaken by local nonprofit organizations have garnered their own share of attention.

Foremost among these is an extraordinary six-hundred-acre wetlands restoration at Tidmarsh Farms, undertaken by the property owners—Evan Schulman, Glorianna Davenport, and their family—along with a host of public and private partners. These included the Natural Resources Conservation Service of the US Department of Agriculture; Mass Audubon; the Town of Plymouth; the US Fish and Wildlife Service, and the Massachusetts Division of Ecological Restoration. Tidmarsh Farms was at the time the largest ecological restoration of a freshwater site ever undertaken in the Northeast. What was previously Tidmarsh Farms is now a wildlife sanctuary owned and managed by Mass Audubon.[2]

Living Observatory, another nonprofit linked to Tidmarsh, is a technology partner in this restoration project. Living Observatory refers to itself as a public interest learning community. The nonprofit plays the key role in "monitoring, interpreting, and learning about how ecosystem function develops following ecological wetland restoration of retired cranberry farms."[3] This educational awareness element of the project is as noteworthy as the restoration work itself.

The organization's livestream monitoring of the restored wetlands has been featured in *Scientific American*.[4] A virtual system of ecological monitoring devices enables visitors to the project's website to hear raindrops falling on leaves or frogs croaking along the restored stream banks. A wide array of sensors and a monitoring network throughout the site make the virtual experience of nature possible. The sensor network at Tidmarsh Wildlife Sanctuary was developed and installed by the MIT Media Lab's Responsive Environments Group, in collaboration with Living Observatory.

Beyond these showcase projects, a loose network of environmental nonprofits exists throughout town to monitor and protect lakes, ponds, watersheds, rare habitat areas, and coastal resources. There are watershed associations, alliances, land trusts, and environmental stewardship organizations. Hundreds of town residents spend thousands of hours pursuing the missions of these organizations. The Friends of Ellisville Marsh, Inc., is one of these, formed in mid-2007.[5]

All things considered, the Town of Plymouth exceeds expectations when it comes to environmental restoration and natural preservation. Citizens who care about the environment and the water resources around them can be found in all corners of the town.

Not Your Garden-Variety Environmentalist

Gould, the director of Plymouth's Department of Marine and Environmental Affairs, deserves much of the credit for Plymouth's environmental awakening. He is not your garden-variety environmentalist. He seems to look kindly on nature, the way one would smile at a close friend or family member. This attitude springs in part from his childhood memories of playing along a remote part of Town Brook. The brook only seems remote because it is hidden in trees down an embankment behind some old houses that line Summer Street, one of the roads leading into town. Many who live in town do not know a brook runs there.

Gould may not think of himself as an environmental activist even though he is the top natural resource officer in town. He keeps a constant eye out for doing what is right for Plymouth. Given the character of the town, that means doing what is right for nature, especially protecting threatened water resources and the ecosystems they support.

Townspeople are lucky to have Gould in this role. He is soft-spoken and patient, quietly persistent in shepherding often-complex projects through a minefield of regulatory rules and grant-funding requirements. He builds relationships easily. Gould has a gift that makes people want to work with him, not because his projects invariably turn out well but because the experience is satisfying and enjoyable. He is not in the least bit self-aggrandizing, even when attention is turned to his impressive string of successful projects.

Gould has patiently won over the most important ally of all—Town Meeting, the ultimate decision-making body in local government. Plymouth Town Meeting is an assemblage of 162 elected representatives, some of whom might be characterized as crusty New Englanders, whose pertinacity can derail projects included in the proposed town budget. But most of the environmental projects make it through, often thanks to Gould. David Gould is highly regarded and underappreciated. His is the guiding hand behind a groundswell of environmental restoration projects in all corners of the town.

Ellisville

Ten miles south of Plymouth's town center sits Ellisville, a historic wayside on the old road to Sandwich on Cape Cod. Traveling from Plymouth to Sandwich in the eighteenth or nineteenth centuries was a journey, not the twenty minutes by car to which modern-day travelers are accustomed. The Cape Cod Canal did not exist, nor did the logjam of tourists making their way across one or the other of the chokepoint bridges to spend a vacation week on the Cape. Travelers in those distant days overnighted at roadside inns in places like Ellisville.

Many who live in Plymouth today do not frequent Ellisville. To those living downtown, the village can seem distant. Recent arrivals to town may not even know Ellisville exists. The name is not found among Plymouth's officially recognized village centers— North Plymouth, Plymouth Center, West Plymouth, Manomet, and Cedarville, although it adjoins the lattermost. People who live in Ellisville more often cross the Sagamore Bridge onto Cape Cod to shop, dine or run errands than trek the ten miles north to Plymouth's town center. For some living in Ellisville, visiting downtown Plymouth is an excuse for a day trip.

Plymouth is made up of many places with archaic names. Some of these are found only on vintage maps but can frequently be heard in everyday conversations among locals. For Plymouth people, these place names are a vital connection to the past, especially for the minority of residents who pride themselves on their direct descendancy from the original Mayflower arrivals. "Native Plymouthians, an Endangered Species" read their bumper stickers.

The old places have names like Chiltonville, Vallerville, Hobs Hole, Jabez Corner, Manter's Point, and Ellisville. Ellisville is named after a family whose seeds were planted in the seventeenth century and whose branches still grow here based on the number of local residents surnamed Ellis. There is Ellisville Road, Ellisville Green, Ellisville Heights, Ellisville Harbor State Park, and, of course, Ellisville Marsh.

Environmental Gem

Ellisville's salt marsh covers about seventy acres. It is hard to precisely measure its area because the edges are constantly shifting, blurred front lines in an ongoing battle between land and sea. To the east the marsh is bounded by a strip of sand as narrow as a hundred yards in places—a barrier beach—which separates the marsh from the sea and defines it in geomorphologic terms. On the marsh's western and northern edges are forested uplands covered by oak and pitch pine. A few fifty-year-old rhododendrons stand prominently on the northern hillside, the last vestiges of homesteads that disappeared long ago.

Henry David Thoreau mentioned Ellisville when he wrote in June 1857 of stopping overnight at Ellis's Tavern by the salt marsh. He recorded in his journal, "I put up at Samuel Ellis's, just beyond the salt pond near by [*sic*], having walked six or seven miles from Manomet through a singularly out-of-the-way region, of which you wonder if it is ever represented in the legislature."[6] Perceiving Ellisville to be distant and remote is not something new.

Thoreau's journal entry continued, "I saw menhaden skipping in the pond as I came along, it being connected to the sea. Ellis, an old man, said that lobsters were plentier than they used to be, that sometimes one got three hundred and upward in a day, and he thought the reason was that they spawned in the cars [*sic*] and so the young were protected from fishes that prey on them."[7] Lobster carrs are clever devices you do not learn about in school or, unless you are lucky, in life. We will come back to them later.

A few rusted iron farm implements sit silently at the edge of the woods by the parking lot at the state park, going mostly unnoticed by visitors intent on making it to the beach at the trail's end near the northern extent of the salt marsh. To the south of the marsh is a good-sized pond, a former cranberry bog that connects to Ellisville Marsh via a small stream where a family of river otters lives and snapping turtles can be seen sunning themselves on logs by the water's edge.

Near the stream and the old bog sits a picturesque, eighteenth-century house, the former Ellis's Tavern mentioned by Thoreau. Today, it is owned and lovingly maintained by Harold and Mary Tincher, who view their home's deep roots with reverence. Walking along the narrow, sandy lane that runs past the white house, one can imagine it as a roadside tavern. Seated at the Tinchers' dining room table, you can almost hear the clatter of a horse-drawn trap bouncing along the rutted lane just outside the window or the heavy clomp of leather boots on the wooden floor in the hall. If only those old walls could share their stories with us.

Ellisville Marsh is the centerpiece of two adjacent wildlife preservation areas, Ellisville Harbor State Park and Shifting Lots Preserve. Both properties are open to the public year round for nature walks and other forms of passive recreation.

The property that became Ellisville Harbor State Park in 1991 had been slated to become a densely packed residential development in the late eighties. Development applications had been filed with the town and appeared likely to move forward despite considerable public outcry. Fortunately, the economy weakened at a critical moment. The developer filed for bankruptcy before ground was broken, and the Commonwealth of Massachusetts stepped in to acquire the hundred-acre property at a price that dramatically understated its developable value.

The property became Ellisville Harbor State Park, a scenic preserve with forested upland, open meadows, a sandy barrier beach, and the northern half of Ellisville Marsh. The Massachusetts Department of Conservation and Recreation (DCR) has described the property as "perhaps the finest vestige along the Massachusetts coastline that reflects early agricultural use."[8]

Visitors follow the park's winding, dirt-and-gravel trail to the sea to catch a view of seals bantering on boulders just offshore or to sunbathe on the narrow sandy beach. They walk unknowingly in the footsteps of Indigenous people who hunted, fished, harvested shellfish, and made tools in this area as far back as thirteen thousand years ago. The park contains remnants of the eighteenth-century Harlow farmstead. The original farmhouse burned down but its replacement stands guard over an old, overgrown farm pond at a western corner of the marsh.

Shifting Lots Preserve, a forty-five-acre parcel which contains the southern half of Ellisville Marsh, is owned by the Wildlands Trust, a Plymouth-based environmental nonprofit. Founded in 1973, Wildlands Trust is one of the largest and oldest regional land trusts in Massachusetts, helping to ensure the protection of eighty-five hundred acres of natural and agricultural lands throughout southeastern Massachusetts. [9]

The families that previously owned this property had been discouraged from continuing to use Ellisville Harbor as a mooring place for lobster boats by regulations put into effect by the state in the 1980s to protect the salt marsh. The landowners had also become frustrated by the willful and wanton behavior of people who drove their four-wheel-drive vehicles onto the beach in what sometimes seemed like an invading swarm of insects brought on by warming weather: on sunny days, as many as fifty cars and trucks crowded onto the narrow barrier beach.

Although the beach and salt marsh had always been private property, some beachgoers ignored the landowners' requests for civility and respectful behavior. They left behind physical reminders of their days spent at the beach. Faced with such intransigence and concerned for the future of Ellisville Marsh, the owners gifted the property to the Wildlands Trust in 2003. It became known as Shifting Lots Preserve.

The transfer deed that accompanied the gift of land was drafted by Ellisville resident and attorney Don Quinn. It included provisions for a beach management plan, protection of wildlife, and erection of physical barriers to permanently exclude vehicles from the beach. It also contained a clause that would assure cooperation in future efforts to maintain the Ellisville Marsh inlet, the salt marsh's life-sustaining connection to the sea.

Quinn is one of those individuals who tackles seemingly impossible tasks with purpose and resolve. In the case of Ellisville Marsh, he had spent years prior to 2003 tracking down dozens of Harlow and Ellis family members who had inherited ownership shares of the property. Over time he was able to purchase all of their interests and consolidate ownership in the Ellisville Harbor Conservation Trust, which, along with the Marsh, Lapham, and Danielson families, transferred the combined property to the Wildlands Trust in 2003.

The families who conveyed the property, as well as those who in other ways enabled permanent protection of the salt marsh, were deeply connected to this place. Protection of the marsh and barrier beach became their legacy, their gift to future generations of Plymouthians and many others who travel from around the world to enjoy this scenic part of the New England coastline. But however foresighted, these actions turned out to be insufficient.

It soon became apparent that protecting the marsh and its surroundings from development and vehicles desecrating the beach would not be enough to restore the natural equilibrium that had been disrupted after agriculture and fishing activities faded away. The natural order of things had been thrown out of kilter by the long-term blockage of the salt marsh inlet.

A Highly Productive Ecosystem

What is the natural order of this special place? To say it is a salt marsh understates its complexity and misrepresents the essence of its being. Ellisville Marsh is a complicated recipe made from saltwater and freshwater ingredients. It is a salt marsh because it is flushed daily by ocean tides. It is an estuary because two freshwater streams and a spring feed into the marsh and from there empty into the bay.

The continuous infusion of salt- and freshwater from these opposing sources maintains the delicate balance of water quality and salinity needed to support a wide spectrum of salt marsh plants, animals, birds, and marine creatures. Many of these species are highly sensitive to their environment. Slight variations in salinity or tidal range can quickly impact their health. And the finely balanced ecosystem on which they depend is inherently fragile.

Ellisville Marsh contains natural resources of incomparable value. Within its banks, it incubates life, nurtures growth, and offers vital habitat. Salt marshes are, it is widely accepted in scientific circles, among the most productive ecosystems on earth. According to the National Oceanic and Atmospheric Administration (NOAA), "They ... provide essential food, refuge, or nursery habitat for more than seventy-five percent of fisheries species, including shrimp, blue crab, and many finfish."[10] These marine species in turn support a wide diversity of other creatures up and down the food chain.

Dr. Ellen Russell, a founding Friends board member and the organization's science adviser, describes in objective terms why coastal marshes are so special:

> Salt marshes have a litany of attributes. They act as "sponges" holding water and dampening the wave energy from coastal storm surge. Their habitat functions as migratory, feeding, breeding, and nursery grounds for shellfish, fish, and waterfowl. They trap plant-based carbon in layers of peat, keeping

it out of the atmosphere. They remove pollutants from our waterways before discharge to the ocean. And they act as buffers to the intrusion of salt water into private wells and septic systems.[11]

Russell's personal and emotional attachment to Ellisville Marsh goes beyond the scientific studies she has conducted here for more than a decade. She speaks to the experience of growing up with the marsh in her backyard:

> What often are not listed by wetlands scientists are the ways an expanse of salt marsh can make us feel, and the emotions it can evoke. The soothing shades of the green grasses and haze of purple when the grasses are in bloom, the way the evening light enhances the golden autumn grasses, these are the subjects of many fine paintings. Add to the visual beauty the briny smell and, sometimes, rotten-egg odors brought on by changes in barometric pressure and tides, and we may be reminded of our mysterious, primordial beginnings. Whether you are fishing from a bank, jumping into an estuary channel, kayaking through the marsh, floating in on a high tide, spotting an osprey just sitting and gazing out, you are communing with the salt marsh and in the process lowering your blood pressure and enhancing your mental and physical well-being.[12]

Two of Russell's children have worked for the Friends as summer interns collecting environmental monitoring data and estimating coverage by saltmarsh cordgrass and other types of vegetation within the confines of one-meter-square plots. Their late grandfather's home sits on a knoll at the edge of the marsh, a site that may eventually become an island accessible only at low tide as sea level continues to rise. The entire family is closely connected to Ellisville Marsh and has been for generations. They have watched as the larger world surrounding the salt marsh has been altered by development and climate change.

Salt marshes are an especially important element in nature's response to the sea level rise associated with climate change. This is no futuristic challenge. Sea level rise is already being recorded in the Gulf of Maine, which includes Cape Cod Bay. Locally, the water has risen higher and higher up Ellisville beach over the past decade, causing erosion of the grassy dunes and coastal bank. This place is a canary in the Atlantic Ocean's coal mine.

Ellisville Marsh is exceptional even among salt marshes. It is recognized by the Commonwealth of Massachusetts as an Area of Critical Environmental Concern (ACEC). Such areas are the most environmentally sensitive and ecologically valuable places in the state and are, not surprisingly, tightly protected by regulatory agencies. Ellisville Harbor is also designated as a Massachusetts Important Bird Area (IBA). Only one other ACEC exists in Plymouth: the Herring River Watershed. Ellisville Harbor is the only Plymouth site to carry both distinctions.[13]

An IBA, according to Mass Audubon, is a site providing essential habitat to one or more species of breeding, wintering, and/or migrating birds. The Cornell Laboratory of Ornithology's online reporting system, eBird, has recorded sightings of 238 distinct species at this birding hot spot.[14] Birders from all over gather with their binoculars and spotting scopes at the curve where Ellisville Road runs along the marsh.

Being a practiced birder is not a prerequisite for becoming spellbound by Ellisville Marsh. The experience of standing at the marsh edge, with or without binoculars, to watch the goings-on can be mesmerizing for anyone who comes to appreciate the vivid, natural kaleidoscope of colors, movements, and sounds.

The Friends periodically sponsor bird walks at the salt marsh to showcase the remarkable variety of birds here. More than fifty people turned out for the Friends' first Welcome Spring! Bird Walk in 2010. Groups led by Becky Harris and Wayne Petersen of Mass Audubon came across a wide variety of birds, migrants and residents, in marsh, beach, meadow, and woodlands habitats. The weather was marvelous and the birds were obliging.

During the walk, Ellisville's first Piping Plover nest of the season was discovered on Ellisville beach and the marsh's recently returned Osprey pair watched over their eggs on the platform that had been placed in the marsh two years earlier. Belted Kingfishers circled over the back marsh, and a recently returned Baltimore Oriole made its colorful appearance on Salt Marsh Lane. Participants learned that Ellisville Marsh and Ellisville Beach are considered significant bird habitats by Mass Audubon, with several Piping Plover pairs (designated as a threatened species by both the United States and Massachusetts) nesting on the beach each spring and summer.

Ellisville Marsh offers a remarkably diverse set of wildlife habitats and foraging areas compressed into postage-stamp size. It has beachfront, an intertidal zone, a flowing stream, low-tide mudflats, fields of tall marsh grass, a saltwater pond, channel banks, sand bars, and cobble ridges, some of which remain dry even on the highest tides. Each has something unique to offer birds and other wildlife: plenty of natural camouflage; a ready food supply in all seasons; well-adapted nesting sites. We hardly notice these as distinct places-within-a-place. Birds certainly do though.

Plovers, sandpipers, and sanderlings use their bills to probe the wet sand left by the receding tide. Great blue herons stand motionless on the channel banks, waiting patiently for unsuspecting fish to come by. Greater Yellowlegs wade in ankle-deep water and probe the muddy bottom. Eiders, buffleheads, mergansers, cormorants, and scoters tuck their heads into the water and dive for fish just offshore.

Migratory shorebirds stop here to rest and recover from epic flights that carry them thousands of miles from wintering grounds in South America to nesting areas above the Arctic Circle. Among these, the black-bellied plover is perhaps the most recognizable. These birds stop at Ellisville Beach on their migration north in May and again on their return south in August to recharge on the plentiful food supplies here. The males sport impressive, black tuxedo bibs and wig-like caps. They resemble pint-size English barristers in formal court attire.

A solitary loon floats near the inlet. He may be the juvenile from a few years back that boldly approached kayakers entering the marsh. A kingfisher loops above the back marsh raising its high-pitched, staccato chatter. Cedar waxwings in the fall and orioles in the spring feed on bittersweet berries and chokecherry growing wild along Salt Marsh Lane. Each knows which part of this special place has what it needs. There is something for everyone here. And not just birds.

Harbor seals lounge on the rocks at low tide off Ellisville beach throughout the winter and spring. Black racers five feet long have been found slithering in the grassy area between the harbor and beach—one even dropped out of an old tire a startled volunteer picked up during cleanup day. Skates glide by in the marsh inlet channel. A striped bass weighing over sixty-three pounds was once caught by a local resident fishing from Ellisville beach. Simply being present here creates unlimited possibilities for witnessing the rich diversity nature has to offer.

Anadromous and catadromous species of fish frequent Ellisville Marsh and the Ellisville estuary. Anadromous fish, those that spend their adult lives at sea but spawn in freshwater, include river herring. The herring run that connects the salt marsh with a freshwater pond a half mile upstream has become impassable, but historical accounts document the presence of river herring here. Catadromous fish, on the other hand, are born in the ocean, live in freshwater, and return to the ocean to spawn. American eel is the only catadromous fish in North America. They, too, are present in Ellisville Marsh. Both fish species depend on the connection between ocean and salt marsh, and between the salt marsh and a freshwater pond, for their populations to survive and grow.

The Ellisville Marsh Inlet

A large stream, or tidal channel, connects Ellisville Marsh with the sea. This is the Ellisville Marsh inlet, the central physical element around which everything in this story revolves. The inlet enables incoming and outgoing tides to flush the salt marsh twice daily. It plays a vital role in maintaining salinity and water quality in the marsh and enables the rising and falling water levels that are essential for sustaining healthy marsh vegetation.

This physical connection between salt marsh and sea has endured for centuries, yet it remains fragile and uncertain. The marsh inlet exists at the pleasure of the sea and is influenced by the weather with all its vagaries. The inlet is also subject to the whims of humans. The Commonwealth of Massachusetts intervened heavy-handedly in 1960, building a hardened structure of boulders on the inlet's north side in an attempt to keep it open by blocking the southward flow of sand along the coast. This produced unintended consequences that we will discuss later.

The Ellisville Marsh inlet is noted in historical accounts written by visitors to Ellisville. A surveyor sent to southeastern Massachusetts in 1791 to explore sites for a possible canal across Cape Cod wrote in his logbook that the Ellisville Marsh inlet in that day was man-made. His entry reads, "Seven miles from Sandwich is Ellis's tavern. . . . At Ellis's is an artificial harbor made by opening a pond. The roots of trees there prove it to be artificial."[15]

The inlet may or may not have been man-made back then. However, it was not located where it is today. The inlet was moved to its current spot by powerful storms that battered the coastline, as they continue to do today. In fact, hand-drawn maps indicate the marsh inlet has shifted locations several times in the past two hundred years.

The surveyor's account goes on to describe in detail how the inlet migrates, a dynamically triggered event we continue to observe in this modern era. Even though he visited Ellisville in the eighteenth century, the surveyor was by no means among the earliest observers. Nor were the Pilgrims, who had arrived almost two centuries earlier.

The Wampanoag

Assuming that the history of Ellisville Marsh began with the sixteenth-century arrival of European traders or the Pilgrims shortly thereafter is naive and ill-informed. Predecessors of the Wampanoag tribe, known as Paleoindians, arrived in the area some thirteen thousand years ago. Although precise historical records of Indigenous people's encampments at or near Ellisville Marsh are not available, the ways in which the Paleoindians migrated suggest that the Ellisville estuary and salt marsh would have been a desirable location. According to Edward L. Bell of the Massachusetts Historical Commission: "The Paleoindian explorers and resident populations entered New England from multiple routes, when initial scouts and later extended family groups made their way around or across the Great Lakes and the Mid-Atlantic regions through the river valleys and mountain cloves of the St. Lawrence, Connecticut, Hudson, and Delaware rivers, but also likely up and down the Atlantic coastal plain. They got around the easternmost areas of Massachusetts using regionally important river drainages—the Ipswich, Merrimack, Mystic, Charles, Neponset, and Taunton rivers—that drain to the coast. Explorative forays established a few large marshalling camps occupied by a considerable number of people. Smaller groups were highly mobile and set up smaller camps."[16]

Melissa (Harding) Ferretti is president and chairperson of the Herring Pond Wampanoag tribe, a tight-knit community of Indigenous people whose presence in the Ellisville Marsh area is well documented. She is an energetic woman, deeply committed to the challenge of recovering her tribe's ancestral homelands, reclaiming the tribal language, and restoring lost cultural traditions. Her flowing blonde hair helped lead the tribal medicine man to bestow on her the name "Golden Dragonfly."

Ferretti speaks warmly of her childhood visits to the spring flowing from the hillside that borders Ellisville Marsh. She and her great aunt, a remarkable tribal elder named Verna May

Harding, would walk the mile or so from their home in Cedarville to the spring, carrying water on their return. Harding had an encyclopedic knowledge of the plants that grew along the old Indian trails. Ferretti recalls that growing at the spring was a bush with white flowers whose blossoms they rubbed on their hands with water, eliciting a sweet aroma like a scented soap.[17]

The Herring Pond Wampanoag, who have also been referred to as Patuxet, Pondville, Manomet, Bournedale, Comassakumkanit, and the Praying Indians, [18] moved their encampment to the Cedarville/Ellisville area between 1616 and 1618 as they fled areas on the South Shore where tribal members were dying from "the plague," including the Manomet section of southern Plymouth.[19] However, given the vitality of Ellisville Marsh for river herring, shellfish, and other food sources, tribal members were undoubtedly present here long before this emergency relocation.

The area surrounding the salt marsh is dotted with Pilgrim and Indian burial grounds and is the locus for the "Great Lot," a 2,400- to 2,600-acre ancestral homeland just west of Ellisville Marsh. An ancient Indian encampment has also been identified within a mile south of the marsh. Old Indian trails crisscross the area, many of which lead directly to Ellisville Marsh. It is likely that the salt marsh itself would have been a central feature of the Wampanoag ancestral homelands.

Early Wampanoag people would have, according to Ferretti, viewed Ellisville Marsh as a sacred place given its abundance of fish and game. The presence of herring in particular would have been a reason to give ceremonial thanks. Tribal members not only ate the fish but also placed one herring beneath every seed they planted. Nothing was wasted. Sustainability did not originate with descendants of the Europeans who colonized Massachusetts Bay but was a fact of life for the Wampanoag. Sustainable fish and game stocks meant survival.

What do the Herring Pond Wampanoag people and their ancestors have in common with twenty-first-century stewards of the salt marsh? They share a deep connection and reverence for a coastal place with extraordinary beauty and rich natural resources. A heightened awareness of the plant and animal life that make up the complex mosaic of the marsh ecosystem. A bias toward minimizing man's footprint and reversing the harmful impacts of development. And an appreciation of a special place that is deeply spiritual. When it comes to Ellisville Marsh, the Friends and the Wampanoag people are kindred spirits. We are connected to this place, and ultimately to one another.

The value of timeless observations such as those of the Wampanoag or the eighteenth-century surveyor are largely lost today. The regulatory process that wraps its protective arms around natural places like Ellisville Marsh focuses on recent, officially documented history. Decisions are dictated by what is contained in permitting dockets and shown on recorded, twentieth-century and twenty-first-century plans.

Regulatory decision-making that relies entirely on recent engineering plans overlooks much of what has been learned over the course of centuries about the dynamics of this salt marsh and its tidal inlet by farmers and fishermen and -women who plied their trades here. Whether it is inherently a salt pond or a salt marsh connected to the sea is even questioned by state agency staffers.[20] Modern-day environmental regulations treat the two differently.

The Importance of Tidal Exchange

A coastal salt marsh exchanges water through its tidal inlet. Seawater is pumped through the marsh's veins by the rising and falling tides. The water level rises and falls with the twice-daily tide cycle. The salt marsh breaks down organic material through decomposition, storing nutrients in its soggy soils and sublayers and ejecting organic detritus to the sea.

A salt marsh's health depends on maintenance of a delicate balance. Nonnative plants and animals invade when the natural system becomes out of kilter and resistance is lowered. The marsh is moody—angry, sad, or bright, reflecting the weather, wind, tides, and a host of other influences. Once you become fully attuned to its mood swings, you can almost feel the marsh's heartbeat.

Maintaining tidal exchange between salt marsh and ocean is essential to the health of the fisheries and wildlife that inhabit the marsh, as well as the birds that use it as a resting stop on their long-haul migrations. The inlet, which physically connects the marsh to the bay, is every bit as vital to a salt marsh as an airway is to the human body. A blocked airway makes it much harder to acquire the oxygen needed to preserve life. So it is with a salt marsh and tidal flows. A blocked inlet makes it more difficult for seawater to flood into and drain out of the marsh.

As tides rise and fall, seawater flows in and out. Smaller channels and creeks distribute the life-giving flow to the far corners of the marsh, inundating almost everything in the low marsh, the areas that flood frequently. An open and direct inlet allows for hydraulically efficient tidal exchange. The entire volume of water corresponding to the tide's changing level comes and goes without being restricted. Once inside the marsh, the water goes where it wants to go based on the slightest elevation differences.

Flooding and draining a salt marsh is like filling and emptying a pool. A large hose is needed. Too narrow a hose and the volume of flow is restricted. Bending the hose into a right angle reduces the flow considerably. When the Ellisville Marsh inlet becomes partially blocked by sand washed in by a storm and bends into a right angle of its own, the water is slowed as it comes and goes.

Ellisville Marsh is flushed by a very large hose indeed. An estimated 50 million gallons flow each way through the salt marsh inlet in a typical, six-hour tide cycle. The water flows at an average rate that exceeds 2,000 gallons per second, capable of filling a 660,000-gallon, Olympic-size swimming pool in five minutes. The flow rate is considerably higher at the peak of the tide cycle.

It can be hard for many of us to relate to water volumes of this magnitude. There is another way to think about it. The volume of water flowing back and forth through the Ellisville Marsh inlet during its two daily tide cycles is an estimated 200 million gallons. This is nearly fifty times the average daily volume needed to supply all 15,000 homes, businesses, and municipal buildings on the town's water system. That water comes from thirteen drinking-water-supply wells scattered around town.

What happens when this all-important marsh inlet becomes blocked by a barrier spit? Beyond a certain point of channel attenuation and flow restriction the water cannot fully drain from the marsh before the tide turns and water begins flowing back in again. And delay in filling or emptying water from a salt marsh matters greatly to the fish and wildlife there.

Understanding the importance of tidal flows is central to understanding the Ellisville Marsh ecosystem. Some wetland plants, including the indicator species *Spartina alterniflora* (salt-marsh cordgrass), cannot tolerate being submerged for too long. They suffer when the water does not fully drain. In effect, the plants begin to drown. Parts of the marsh stagnate and become brackish, making them more vulnerable to invasive plants taking hold.

Die-off of vegetation has scarred the back parts of Ellisville Marsh. Although the exact cause or causes of the problem are not known with scientific certainty, tidal flow restriction is believed to be a contributing factor. Periodic storms cause formation of a blocking spit that diverts the tidal inlet south along Ellisville Beach and lengthens the path the water must follow. Eventually, the water cannot fully drain from the marsh when the tide goes out. This causes marsh cordgrass stems to remain submerged for longer periods than the vegetation can tolerate.

Old-timers who fished and operated their lobster boats out of the former harbor have counseled that the most hydraulically efficient profile for the Ellisville Marsh inlet is "straight, narrow, and deep." This configuration enables the daily process of tidal flooding and draining to scour the channel and inlet, flushing out silt and sediment that has drifted in.

A lobsterman like the late Al Marsh would know. He and the other lobster boat captains used to deftly maneuver their boats through the narrow inlet into the shallow harbor on the high tide and make them fast to long oak staves driven deep into the bottom along one side of the channel. This practice ensured that when the tide went out their boats would rest on their sturdy keels and not "keel over."

The Inlet Becomes Blocked

Ellisville fishermen and lobstermen maintained the salt marsh inlet and channel throughout the twentieth century until the state enacted new, more restrictive regulations in 1982.[21] The new rules prohibited them from continuing the practice without costly and difficult-to-obtain permits. This sudden change of fortune was ironic since it was a Massachusetts state agency that in 1960 built the rock jetty on the northern side of the Ellisville Marsh inlet that contributes to inlet blockages when major storms pound the coastline.

In the latter half of the twentieth century, building rock jetties and groins to alter the movement of sand along the coast was thought to be beneficial. However, building hardened structures on the beach and placing stone revetments at the base of the coastal bank, both of which became widespread practices across the United States, produced unexpected and unwanted consequences.

As geo-coastal engineers would learn after years of experience, beach structures failed to solve the problem of sediment movement. Instead, they created new problems. By blocking sediment from its natural drift along the coast, these hardened structures ended up starving downdrift beaches and, in some places, accelerating erosion of the coastal bank. At Ellisville Marsh the rock jetty alongside the channel interferes with the natural process and periodically impacts tidal exchange between ocean and marsh.

Marsh, the lobsterman and Navy veteran, and his family

owned a significant part of Ellisville Marsh in the 1980s. He maintained the salt marsh inlet so he could bring his boat into the harbor. In 1986 Marsh became the subject of a regulatory enforcement action and was fined several thousand dollars by the Massachusetts Department of Environmental Protection (MassDEP) for performing minor and routine maintenance of the Ellisville Marsh inlet. Here was an unmistakable sign that the commonwealth intended to enforce its newly enacted regulations. The action stopped work on the inlet for nearly two decades, by which time tidal flows had become severely restricted and native marsh vegetation had begun to die off.

Lobstering boats were no longer able to reach the harbor inside the marsh, bringing to a bitter end an era of small- and family-scale fishing that had endured for centuries.[22] Regulatory enforcement related to the Ellisville Marsh inlet was to be repeated in 2005 when the MassDEP brought another legal action, this time against local homeowner Vlad Hruby, who the agency claimed had also performed unauthorized work at the inlet.

For several hundred years, farmers and fishermen had maintained the Ellisville Marsh inlet. They kept the inlet open because it was in their commercial self-interest to do so. But in the process, they had preserved the vitality of the marsh's natural system. Bureaucratic action to protect a property that had only recently become designated as an ACEC brought a sudden end to that. More than a hundred years of fishing and lobstering out of Ellisville Marsh ground to a halt.

In fact, designating Ellisville Harbor as an ACEC virtually ensured it would be cut off from nature. Nearly twenty years would pass before work could resume to restore tidal flows and to begin bringing the damaged marsh back to its earlier state of health. The marsh's connection with the sea had been broken, and it would take a Herculean effort by a band of local crusaders to restore it. But the damage had already been done. Ellisville Marsh was no longer the place it once was.

CHAPTER 2

How It Is, How It Was

⌒

ELLISVILLE MARSH AND ITS barrier beach are mostly quiet these days. In summer the gate to the sandy parking lot that sits just behind the dune is closed to protect shorebird nests on the beach. In winter the cold wind off the bay keeps all but the most determined beach walkers away.

Winter is when the finest sand piles up on the beach. By summer it has been scoured away again, leaving mostly small cobble and pebbles by the water's edge, tough on the feet. Young children seem to manage though. Their unbridled enthusiasm outweighs the discomfort of walking barefoot across an expanse of small rocks.

Swimming and sunbathing are the modern-day pastimes here. The water is always cold in Cape Cod Bay, especially on east-facing beaches like Ellisville's. But there is a secret to swimming here in the summer when the air and water conditions make immersion tolerable. One waits for a high tide with an easterly wind. On the fortunate occasions when these conditions are met, the topmost, sun-warmed layer of water drifts into the shallows near shore. On these rare days one can levitate for an hour or more in the water's warm embrace.

On other days it takes no small amount of courage to go in because swimming comes with a shock. For brave souls who make it all the way in, there is exhilaration, sometimes accompanied by an uncontrolled burst of laughter that can be heard down the beach—it can be a bracing experience.

Ralph Casale is the uncrowned king of Ellisville Beach in this regard. He makes his way to the shore most summer afternoons in his swim trunks and signature plastic crocs and, without fanfare, wades into the bay for what is typically a brief dunk. One imagines that at least once in his life Casale has participated in one of those polar bear plunges on New Year's Day. Once refreshed he can be found holding court in a molded plastic beach chair, one of those community items no one seems to know who actually owned to begin with.

Fishing boats are no longer moored in the old harbor. Although the marsh may still be considered a harbor of safe refuge, no boat of any size can make it through the silted channel these days.[1] Entering in a kayak is challenging enough, even at high tide when the channel is at its deepest. Old photos showing boats moored to staves along the channel or the fish houses at the edge of the salt marsh evoke curiosity rather than familiarity. Memories of activities that took place here have not been completely erased though. They are like jewels in a treasure chest, buried but not entirely forgotten.

A photo was recently unearthed by Friends member Betsy Puckett, whose family has lived in Ellisville for generations. The quiet winter scene pictured is a reminder of the way Ellisville Marsh once was. According to Puckett, "This photo was taken around 1960 during a very high tide. There was a road between the fish houses and the high tide mark that is covered with water in the photo. My dad, Walter Pleadwell, was friends with the lobsterman Bob Glass, and both my sister Susan Pleadwell and I went out with Bob as he pulled his pots. To go out on the boat you had to work, which meant pegging lobsters, a frightful job for a 10- or 11-year-old. And what an incredible memory and experience it was."[2]

Al Marsh, longtime Friends member and adviser, commented, "Bob Glass was my stepbrother. One fish house belonged to Joe

Morse Jr. The other belonged to my father, Percy Marsh, later shared with Bob Glass. I built a small addition in 1957 after I left the Navy. They were older than me but we always had good times together, mostly at the harbor." For so many who called this place home, fishing defined Ellisville Harbor and made it the center of a community that respected nature and understood how to coexist with it.

The old-timers' stories paint a picture of the way things were in a place that is no longer what it was: farmers harvesting marsh hay, rotating the best plots among their families through the centuries; fishermen applying unconventional methods to net an abundance of fish where the inlet opened wide to the sea; lobster carrs floating just beneath the surface a few hundred yards offshore; local teenagers raking sea moss off boulders at low tide in a summer rite of passage.

Past generations had a way of life that revolved around and depended on the salt marsh. Locals viewed this natural resource through the lens of necessity. It was their livelihood. They cared for the marsh as though their lives depended on it, for at times they did.

Fishing and Shellfishing

As far back as records exist, Ellisville Marsh was the center of farming, fishing, clamming, and lobstering for the tight-knit community that surrounded it. It was undoubtedly so for the Indigenous people who came before. In good weather or bad, local residents appeared at the marsh on a daily basis to farm marsh hay and set their fishing nets for river herring and larger fish.

Old accounts speak of locals cutting holes through the ice in winter, not for fishing but to spear eels in the muddy marsh bottom. Several odd-looking tridents with barbed and backward-bent prongs were unearthed by an excavator the Friends had brought in for inlet maintenance. They turned out to be tools used to spear eels, used as far back as colonial times.

More conventional forms of fishing were also prevalent here. Ernest Clifton Ellis recounts in his *Reminiscences of Ellisville* that Thomas Clark Harlow, a descendant of Thomas Harlow (1686–1746), whose house sat just beyond the western perimeter of the marsh until it burned down in 1938, "used to take quantities of alewives which he salted, cured and smoked."[3] Ellis noted that the herring went upstream to Savery Pond to spawn, a passage no longer possible because of blockages along the course of the old herring run. Catching the herring was practical and straightforward. As the tide ebbed, Harlow and others would stretch their seine nets across the main channel as the herring made their return to the bay and haul them out.

Ellisville Marsh was also one of several sites in southeastern Massachusetts and on Cape Cod where fishing was accomplished with fixed nets called "fishing weirs" around the turn of the nineteenth century.[4] Sagamore and Barnstable are also mentioned as sites of fishing weirs in historical documents. The fishing weir in Ellisville was operated just offshore near the mouth of the marsh inlet from around 1890 until the early 1920s. According to Ellis, "They were formed by a series of long oak poles set in the ocean floor about three-quarters of a mile off shore upon which the nets were hung to trap the fish. Percy Marsh and I helped set the poles one spring and attached the nets for the season. . . . The most marketable fish caught were mackerel, codfish, some small quantities of mixed varieties, and for a few years, large quantities of a variety named weakfish or squiteag. There were as many as 100 barrels a haul, a haul being one daily trip to the weir to take the fish from the net."[5]

Grainy black-and-white photographs from the period show fish thrashing in the nets as men hauled them into shallow-bottomed wooden boats. Some of the fish were reportedly quite large, including bluefin tuna weighing up to five hundred pounds. Fishermen at the time called these "horse mackerel" as they were considered unfit for human consumption and fed to livestock instead.[6]

The big fish that were still close to shore in the twentieth century are much farther out to sea now. This is sad news for those who still cast their fishing lines off the stone jetty and rock groins in Ellisville. Late Ellisville resident Ron Dolan was so proud of the enormous striped bass he caught in the 1980s fishing from the beach that he handed out souvenir pictures for almost thirty years! It is hard for anyone in the neighborhood to forget the photo of Dolan and his big striper, which weighed in at nearly sixty-four pounds and was almost as tall as he was.

Clams were once plentiful as well. Inside Ellisville Marsh, a sand shoal or island that appears at very low tides in the old harbor is still replete with soft-shelled clams, more commonly known as "steamers." Lest anyone get the idea to harvest some, this area is permanently off-limits to shellfishing by order of the Plymouth Harbormaster, part of a long-term strategy to maintain healthy populations of the bivalves.

Ellisville Marsh, its barrier beach, and its tidal flats have always been a nursery for all manner of shellfish. The much larger and tougher hard-shell clams known as "surf clams" or "sea clams" used to be abundant as well. They could be found until about five years ago shallowly buried in the sand flats at low tide. You could stub your toe on one when walking on the sandbars. Today it requires patience to find a single surf clam.

Vlad Hruby is a surf clam finder of local renown. He wades patiently around in shallow water at low tide looking for some subtle indication on the bottom that foretells the presence of these buried clams. Is the clue a twist of gray sand? A slight mound? Only Hruby can find them. He has a heightened awareness. A deep, intuitive sense. A connection. Even when he has shown the rest of us the telltale pattern we are unable to replicate his feat. For Hruby, clam hunting is a form of mindfulness therapy.

Clams, it turns out, are full of possibilities. One summer game that enthralls young children suffering from bouts of boredom is clam racing. Two clams are stood up side by side in wet sand with their sharp edge facing downward. The clam that completely reburies itself first is the winner.

During the race, all of the action takes place out of view below the clam and there appear to be no moving parts, so the whole thing mystifies unenlightened observers. Using its siphon, the clam is able to liquefy the solid sand below it into a quicksand-like substance that enables the weight of its shell to gradually slide downward. The game teaches children, and some adults as well, a valuable trait: patience. Sadly, the operation of large vessels known as "clam dredgers" just offshore has helped to decimate the population of surf clams in Ellisville's intertidal zone, that special place that exists between the high and low watermarks.

Systematic Destruction of the Sea Floor

Commercial clam dredging is, unfortunately, no game. Specially equipped ships that dredge for sea clams off Ellisville and elsewhere inflict enormous damage on the marine environment. Large metal boxes called "dredges" are pulled along the sea floor behind the ship. Water jets excavate a trench along the bottom, dislodging surf clams and uprooting everything around them.

The dredgers operate close to shore in Ellisville for weeks, sometimes months at a time. Using GPS technology they sweep back and forth, taking virtually every clam that lies within in the grid pattern. It is the systematic decimation of a marine ecosystem.

Ellisville residents have reported clam-dredging vessels to the Massachusetts Environmental Police when they are seen to be operating illegally, either at night or in water shallower than regulations specify. Little has been done to address this active threat to the marine environment however.

In 2017 the Massachusetts Lobstermen's Association filed complaints that mobile lobster gear was being torn up by the clam dredge vessels. After several public hearings and a written comment period, the Massachusetts Division of Marine Fisheries (DMF) implemented a temporary two-month ban on clam dredging close to the shore in Ellisville. But that was the extent of enforcement action. Ironically, DMF officials had told the Friends emphatically during the permitting process to reopen the blocked Ellisville Marsh inlet that any impacts to the Ellisville eelgrass bed even indirectly attributable to inlet maintenance would be cause for immediate permit suspension or revocation. In stark contrast, clam-dredging vessels operate in close proximity to, and have occasionally appeared to penetrate, the same eelgrass bed with impunity. Enforcement of environmental regulations to protect sensitive natural resources like eelgrass is inconsistent. There is a double standard. It matters who you are.

Learning from an Old Lobsterman

Other than the clam dredgers operating offshore, lobstering is one of the only remaining activities with commercial purpose in the immediate vicinity of Ellisville Marsh. The boats no longer operate from the harbor itself. Lobstermen such as the late Al Marsh and his father, Percy, were among a handful of locals who moored their boats in Ellisville Harbor for decades.

Percy Marsh began lobstering in the years after the fishing weirs were given up, and Al finally pulled his boat out around 1987. That was when he was faced with the costly task of developing engineering plans for regulatory permits that maintenance of the inlet required after 1982. As noted, Al Marsh was the target of an enforcement action by the commonwealth in the mideighties when he sought to simply continue the minimal channel maintenance that had been ongoing for decades to maintain access to the old harbor.

A moment in January 2011 imprinted Al Marsh in our memories. The eighty-two-year-old lobsterman stood quietly atop the channel bank near the inlet, watching intently as the excavator ripped into the final sand wall holding back the impounded seawater. When the water was finally liberated and made its exuberant escape into the bay, tears welled in Marsh's eyes, revealing the depth of his bond and kinship with this place. *His* place. It was as though he was witnessing a beloved family member finally emerge from years of hardship and suffering. A lifetime of experience was compressed into that moment. Those standing close by felt the emotional waves radiating from Marsh. Inspiration in its rawest form comes from moments like this.

Marsh has described with his own words what life was like for a lobsterman working out of Ellisville Harbor from the forties onward. His "Ellisville History," a copy of which he gave to the Friends shortly before his death in September 2020, is contained in Appendix A. Lobstering was hard work performed in often dangerous conditions, even when operating close to shore. Fourteen- to sixteen-foot dories were rowed out to the lobstering boats where they were anchored offshore. The younger men like Marsh opted for boats with small cabins which his father Percy called "ice cream stands." Their skiffs were square at the stern with a five- or six-horsepower outboard. To an earlier generation of lobstermen, use of an outboard motor or protective cabin might have seemed soft.

To suggest that the newer generation of Ellisville lobstermen in any way led an easier life would be overlooking the conditions in which they invariably operated when the weather turned cold. The lobstermen kept their boats in the water until mid-December, well after the first winter nor'easter typically hits. The sea this late in the year can take on a malevolent personality. Many New England fishing boat captains over the years have learned the hard way to heed gale warnings.

The boats the lobstermen used to set and pull their traps were typically twenty-eight feet in length and fairly narrow beamed, eight or nine feet in the early days. The lobsters they caught were sold in a variety of ways. A large boat known as a "smack" came down from Boston to buy lobsters from fishermen and -women all along the coast.

The lobsters were more commonly taken by truck off the beach and out to the main road via Salt Marsh Lane. It is hard to visualize how trucks hauling fish could possibly have traversed Salt Marsh Lane. These days the dirt track is overgrown and at times nearly impassable as bittersweet, dense poison ivy patches, and wild grapevines close in from both sides.

Lobsters were stored in large wooden crates called lobster "carrs." Each carr was divided into compartments for lobsters of different sizes. Al Marsh's "Ellisville History" describes the construction of the lobster carr and its ingenious method of anchoring. Friends board member and past president Jack Scambos recalls the hazard that lobster carrs posed to small boats from when he was an Ellisville teenager. Because the carr was anchored just below the surface, it could easily be rammed by a sailboat or small power boat, causing damage to the hull. Scambos's youthful sailing days brought him into many near collisions with these underwater menaces.

The lobster carr was made of rough spruce timber. It measured about 12 feet by 4 feet by 18 inches and was divided into three compartments to separate different-size lobsters. These carrs would be anchored about three hundred yards from the beach and served as a holding pen for the daily catch. A dip net could be used at the carr to bail out the lobsters into boxes where they were covered with burlap and brought to shore to be trucked to market. Or if a buyer could be contacted a day ahead, the carr would be towed in about a half hour before high tide and unloaded into boxes and placed right onto the buyer's truck. The former Snow Inn in Harwich Port purchased a great many Ellisville lobsters.

Although the lobstermen were apparently quite savvy about marketing their product to get a fair price, the market sometimes collapsed entirely. As Marsh recalled, "During the Great Depression, the market for lobsters was almost nonexistent. My father at one time had two full carrs and finally sold the entire amount for a nickel apiece regardless of size!" (see Appendix A).

How the lobster boats were moored in the old harbor is a look back at an earlier way of life at Ellisville Marsh. Deep holes were dug along the north side of the marsh channel, using barrels as cofferdams to keep water out while the area inside was being excavated. After a hole of sufficient depth had been cleaned out and the gravely sand removed, a long oak pole was placed in the hole and driven down as far as possible.

Stabilized with guy lines, the poles enabled the boats to be tied up on one side so that they did not tip over when the tide went out. All in all, the method of mooring was an ingenious system whose necessity was created by the continuously rising and falling water levels in the salt marsh channel. The difference between low and high tides at Ellisville can be as great as fourteen vertical feet. Marsh recalled, "Once tied up inside the harbor the boats were in a very safe location until colder weather came and ice formed in the harbor." The harbor freezes over less frequently these days, but one can still see the broken stumps of some of the mooring poles half a century later.

By the late eighties, owing in large part to the new restrictions that had been imposed on activities at Ellisville Marsh, lobstering was winding down. More than a century of productive use of Ellisville Harbor came to an end. The powerful connections Al Marsh and his fellow lobstermen had built with the salt marsh began to fade. But these old-timers' stories kept them alive.

The lobstermen had also helped keep the marsh itself alive. An aerial photograph taken in 1987 showed a healthy-looking salt marsh. More recent images reveal ten acres of bare mudflats in the back marsh where the cordgrass has died back. Ellisville's lobstermen were apparently doing something right.

Marsh noted in his "Ellisville History" that the current rock jetty just north of the Ellisville inlet on the state park property was built in 1960. The channel at that time could accommodate a thirty-six-foot boat with a three-foot draft at high tide. However, after its first ten years or so, the jetty had stockpiled enough sand on its north side that subsequent storms began to wash it over the top and into the channel, which increased the likelihood of channel blockage. When this happened, contractors were hired in the spring to clear and straighten the channel. This maintenance approach is much the same as the Friends follow today, subject to a raft of local, state, and federal permits.

Inlet Maintenance Grinds to a Halt

The commonwealth began requiring engineering plans and permits to maintain the Ellisville Marsh inlet around 1986, as noted. The cost to successfully navigate through the permitting process was generally seen as prohibitive for an individual or small group of residents. Hruby and contributing neighbors paid $68,000 in 2002–3 to gain the needed permits for his emergency inlet work. It cost the Friends almost the same amount when the group pursued its own inlet maintenance permits in 2008–10. But should permits even have been required?

The official map that defines the boundaries of the Ellisville Harbor Area of Critical Environmental Concern (ACEC) clearly shows the Ellisville Marsh tidal inlet as excluded from the ACEC. The only plausible explanation for this carve-out is that the drafters expected that the inlet would be maintained by lobster boat operators going forward.[7] Nonetheless, the question of whether the marsh inlet falls inside or outside the ACEC became a bone of contention between Ellisville residents and state officials that has never been fully resolved. An earlier wetlands protection order that had been issued in 1981 by the secretary of the Massachusetts Department of Environmental Management also explicitly recognized maintenance dredging of the Ellisville Marsh inlet by listing among allowed activities "maintenance dredging of existing channels and marine facilities provided that such maintenance dredging shall not increase the scope of the initial dredge area."[8]

However, the presence of this seemingly friendly regulatory language would prove to be of little practical value. State agencies vigorously enforced a ban on inlet maintenance even though it appeared to be an allowed activity. Perhaps they anticipated that a handful of local lobstermen would not have the stomach or financial resources to fight enforcement actions. If so, they were correct.

Al Marsh ended up throwing in the towel. Whenever the subject of the state's actions came up in conversations, even thirty years later, he expressed bitterness over the turn of events that had led to his banishment from the harbor he loved. Who outside of bureaucratic circles could blame him? Bureaucratic overreach had ended more than a century of local efforts to maintain the Ellisville Marsh inlet and channel so that fishing boats could enter and leave the harbor.

An Ellisville Rite of Passage

Lobstering was by no means the only commercial activity that used to take place in Ellisville. Marsh notes in his "Ellisville History" that locals began harvesting sea moss in Ellisville in the 1940s. People had always taken advantage of the natural resources that were available here: American eels and river herring, followed by larger ocean fish, lobsters and shellfish, and later, a form of red algae called sea moss. Some of these activities go back thousands of years.

Along with the earlier fishing weirs, sea mossing was an industry that, while also pursued in several other South Shore towns, helped define Ellisville's unique character. Also known as "Irish moss," the algae grew on submerged rocks just offshore and could be harvested for carrageenan, a valuable substance it contains.

Roger Janson, a Friends member who still lives within walking distance of the marsh, worked summers in the 1960s while in high school harvesting sea moss for Eastern Sea Moss, a company in nearby Kingston. According to Janson, sea moss was a three- to five-inch flat, fanlike growth on the boulders within a few hundred yards of shore that could only be collected in the few hours surrounding low tide. As a result, the work schedule shifted on a daily basis.

Young men and women from the surrounding area would show up at the harbor to walk flat-bottomed wooden dories owned by the company out through the shallow channel into the bay. Using a twelve-foot, long-handled rake with a bronze head made up of closely spaced tines held at a forty-five-degree angle, they would stand in the boat, one foot on the bottom and the other braced against the gunwale, and reach several feet down into the water to scrape the sea moss off the rocks. Janson still has his sea mossing rake more than fifty years on.

In a good day, a single person could harvest more than one thousand pounds of sea moss to bring back to the harbor to be weighed and loaded on a truck. For this, he or she would be paid the princely sum of two to three cents per pound, or twenty to thirty dollars for the day. Over the course of a single season, the oak handle of the rake would be entirely worn through by its constant heavy rubbing against the gunwale.

Sea mossing was, according to Janson, almost a rite of passage for Ellisville teenagers. The harvesters, mostly boys, did the hard work and often brought neighborhood girls along for the day. Once in a while they were rewarded with a close-up sighting of a whale or some other marvel of nature. The teenagers' names still ring familiar in Ellisville, as many still live in the area.

Plymouth historian Jim Baker has written a short piece entitled, "Sea Moss in Plymouth: Greg White Remembers," which describes in detail the techniques used to collect, dry, transport, and process the harvested material.[9] The senior mosser named in his account was, coincidentally, Roger Janson's brother, Bob.

What exactly is the constituent of sea moss that was valuable to extract? Carrageenan has been used in traditional cooking for hundreds of years, often as a thickener or gelling agent in ice cream, cottage cheese, nondairy milks, jelly, pudding, and infant formula. In the past, it was also used to clarify beer and added to beverages, purportedly for its health benefits. Baker discusses its uses, and how they changed over time, in some detail.

There are various explanations for why sea mossing faded away. Dessert recipes and tastes changed. Less costly substitutes became available. Cheaper labor in other countries was difficult to compete with. Notwithstanding any of this, there seems to be less sea moss growing on the rocks off Ellisville Beach these days.

Youthful Views

Sea mossing and helping out on the lobster boats were not the only ways in which younger people came to have a connection with Ellisville Marsh. Jack Scambos is a relative newcomer to Ellisville. His family owns a summer cottage on Lookout Point built by his grandfather sixty-five years ago. His poignant views on the importance of natural places were shaped by growing up next to the marsh:

> Some of my best Ellisville memories surround the harbor. It was a unique environment for kids to grow up in. There were always interesting happenings at the marsh inlet. Most memorable, the three lobster boats I can remember as a child—always there, always reliably leaving and arriving unseen. Regardless of weather, darkness of night, or other distractions, these three boats had to leave and arrive at a specific interval if they were to make it in and out of the harbor. The commitment, the fortitude, and the courage of these men definitely made a mark.
>
> If the weather was to be fair, the three would moor out front of the harbor in a line across the horizon that became the defining view of my childhood summers at Ellisville. Close behind the vessel moorings were the storage bins for the captured live lobsters. These heavy wooden crates were suspended by some flotation just below the surface of the water, designed to store lobsters in the cold ocean water. As a small boater, these were very dangerous if you

hit them, likely capsizing your boat and landing you next to a big, underwater floating crate. It was about the size of a car and quite ominous looking, lurking just a few inches below the surface. We loved to fish, but if you got too close to the lobster "carrs" you would immediately catch a dogfish (like a small sand shark), a sculpin, or worse a goosefish—all wasted catch and too scary to haul into your boat to remove the hook. It all added to a unique foreboding that typically kept us and our exploits far from these storage bins—just the way the lobstermen wanted it as they typically contained a couple of weeks' worth of catch.

Inside the harbor was also an unusual and wild-seeming place. The three fishing shacks that lined the marsh were in pretty poor condition. They still retained the remnants of their earlier life—all the hand-lines of wound "COD line," a very heavy, cotton line that got stiff until soaked by water. All sorts of abandoned—or so I thought—fishing paraphernalia from hundreds of lead weights and rusty hooks to broken rods and gaffs of all shapes and sizes. Most unique was a tub full of tar that the older kids teased was for "tar and feathering" bad, younger kids. . . . In fact, it was pitch for repairing the old wooden dories or skiffs and work boats that plied the harbor for everything from flounder and mackerel to sea moss.

The lobster carrs, now dry and empty, were eventually no longer needed due to an increasing demand for fresh lobster and improvements in refrigerated transport and storage. The carrs became the first "bar" for the kids of Ellisville, forming the perfect table top away from the prying eyes of our parents.

Now, having come of age and with our own boats and cars, the harbor allowed easy launch and retrieval of small boats, shelter from storms, and some excellent clamming and fishing. The place was teeming with life—crabs, school stripers, flounder, the occasional shark, but always changing, always incredibly beautiful.

On Halloween of 1991, the year I turned 31, the harbor and marsh experienced a catastrophic change. The "Perfect

Storm" permanently altered the ecosystem of this jewel. This led me to take on one of the longest personal quests of my life: To help restore the marsh and beach to its rightful condition.[10]

Scambos became a founding director of the Friends of Ellisville Marsh in 2007 and has remained on the organization's board since. He served as president for several years and continues in a key leadership role. When asked in 2021 whether he planned to continue on the board for another term, Scambos replied, "I'm still in, until it is, or I am, finished."

Ellisville old-timers and longtimers have deeply influenced the work of revitalizing Ellisville Marsh and what the Friends are doing and why. But the younger generation has also offered its perspective, as expressed in end-of-summer reflections by the Friends' 2015 environmental monitoring intern, Abby Foley, who went on to graduate from the University of New Hampshire (UNH):

> The tasks I had to accomplish throughout the summer included deploying data loggers in three locations to measure tidal elevations, surveying vegetation plots in the marsh, and entering data to add to a portfolio of records from past summers. The morning I deployed the bay logger the water was freezing and I had to use goggles and a mask to see underwater in order to screw the stilling well containing the logger to an anchor. That morning there were hundreds of starfish I had fun observing out front. I also found a huge striper head on the beach, which I took home intending to dissect. I think it is still in our freezer. . . . Another day, I put a stilling well and logger inside an old, unused lobster trap buried under rocks and seaweed in the channel. When I removed this logger at the end of the summer I had quite a surprise. I pulled the stilling well out of the trap and a huge eel that had made the sheltered trap its home slithered out and startled me! The last logger and stilling well I placed was in the marsh.

While we were out there putting a new logger in I had to dive deep in a channel with goggles to try to retrieve a lost logger from last summer that was stuck fast in marsh mud.

The vegetation survey work was a learning experience for me. By the end of the summer I could identify most herbaceous marsh plants, which will surely help with my aquatic botany class I am taking next semester. I learned how to navigate the marsh and avoid the treacherous quicksand-like mud. The field experience is especially valuable to me and I hope to continue applying what I have learned in my marine science classes at UNH.[11]

This young fifth-generation resident of Ellisville, after delving deeply into nature for a summer, had become intimately connected. Such connections with nature are held for generations in a family's DNA.

Grace Pleadwell was one of the Friends' staunchest supporters before passing away at ninety-seven. Her attachment to Ellisville Marsh was long-standing and close. Grace had been coming to Ellisville since the mid-1930s when she met her husband, Walter (now deceased). Walter's father had built a cottage abutting the marsh in 1922. Grace loved to walk the beach and marsh. In the fall, when the flowers were in full bloom, Grace and her daughter Susan would pick a few sprigs of beach heather. Put in a vase, they would last the winter as dried flowers. The spirits of those who lived in this place, who loved this place, still walk among the wildflowers that grow on the beach and among the dunes.

Chapter 3
....

Plants under Siege

⌒

AT FIRST GLANCE, ELLISVILLE Marsh may seem to be little more than a field of tall grass swaying in the wind. However, the salt marsh and surrounding upland area harbor an incredible diversity of plant life—more than 150 species.

Plants are vital to the health of ecosystems, especially in a salt marsh. They convert carbon dioxide to oxygen in the earth's greenhouse. They provide food and habitat for a wide range of creatures. Without a healthy and diverse population of plants, the ways in which the marsh supports wildlife cannot be sustained.

New England salt marshes harbor a vast diversity of native plants that flower during different seasons. They have wonderfully evocative names—seaside cinquefoil, saltmarsh bulrush, sea lavender, seaside angelica, saltmarsh aster, glasswort, seaside plantain, saltmarsh false foxglove, seabeach sandwort, saltmarsh sand-spurrey, to name a few.

Each of these has been found at Ellisville Marsh by botanists Irina Kadis and Alexey Zinovjev. This highly knowledgeable pair has made exceptional contributions to the Friends' understanding of the flora in and around the salt marsh. Kadis worked as curatorial assistant at Harvard's famed Arnold Arboretum in Boston for many years. Without fanfare or public recognition, Kadis and Zinovjev tirelessly assist nonprofits around Massachusetts in developing inventories of plant species that exist on their respective properties.

The pair's knowledge of indigenous and nonnative species is encyclopedic. They are to the plants of Ellisville Marsh and its surrounding upland what seasoned Mass Audubon and Manomet bird experts are to the Ellisville Important Bird Area. Kadis and Zinovjev catalogued 158 plant species during site visits to Ellisville Marsh over the space of just a few days.[1] About fifty of these are nonnative to Massachusetts and about two dozen are invasive, hostile invaders that aggressively displace other species and reduce overall plant diversity. A silent war is being waged at the salt marsh.

What plant was of greatest concern when the project to revitalize Ellisville Marsh was launched? Poison ivy perhaps? Three shiny leaves. Poison ivy lurks everywhere in southeastern Massachusetts and on Cape Cod: in the forests, on the beaches, ringing wild blueberry patches, clinging to the steep slopes of the coastal bank. If Cape Cod were to designate an official plant, one would be hard-pressed not to consider poison ivy. Who among us has not learned the hard way to avoid this plant that wants to teach you a lesson by making your life miserable?

Warming temperatures brought on by climate change have produced an even more virulent form of the plant that some call "super poison ivy." Elevated carbon dioxide levels in the atmosphere promote the growth of poison ivy plants that produce more urushiol, the oil that gets on your skin and causes an allergic reaction and wretched skin rash. But this plant, it turns out, is not a culprit in the decline of New England salt marshes.

In fact, poison ivy is native to the eastern United States and has been with us for a very long time. It provides food and shelter for wildlife. It protects wildlife areas from human intrusion. The plant plays a role in the natural scheme of things, irksome as that may be for active, outdoors people. In fact, only humans suffer from poison ivy. We simply need to accept that it is a player in our natural surroundings and avoid it. Some of the other plants in and around Ellisville Marsh are far more malicious, as the Friends learned.

The plants to worry about have their own memorable names: common reed, spotted knapweed, common wormwood or mugwort, and Japanese knotweed, among others. These plants arrived inauspiciously (some deliberately introduced, others inadvertently) and began displacing native plants, slowly at first, then at an accelerating rate. Many originated in Europe or Asia, but other ferocious invaders, as Kadis refers to them, such as black locust or Carolina fanwort, are native to the East Coast.

The more aggressive invaders are beyond antisocial—they employ malicious tactics to gain ground, literally as well as figuratively. Most of these plants have little usefulness in the overall ecosystem. Some have very low nutritional value and are shunned as a food source by wildlife. Once they become established, though, they can be nearly impossible to eradicate.

Unfortunately, many invasive plants are also attractive. Homeowners knowingly or unknowingly allow these plants to flourish in their yards, along property boundaries and in fields. Some, like beach rose, or *Rosa rugosa*, are popular as garden and landscape elements. People gather spotted knapweed to put in a vase, likely dispersing the seeds on their way home. It is no wonder that so many are enchanted by this flowering plant— the plant belongs to the daisy or aster family, which includes sunflower and a multitude of well-known garden flowers.

The sandy parking area at Shifting Lots Preserve is edged by an impenetrable thicket of intertwined vines: Oriental bittersweet and porcelain berry. Both plants are invasive and spread aggressively. They also present themselves attractively. Porcelain berries start off white and gradually change color to artistic mixes of pink, turquoise, and black as the growing season passes. Birds are drawn to its colorful berries as a food source and spread the seeds. Both porcelain berry and Oriental bittersweet are banned for sale or propagation in Massachusetts. However, both are still found as old plantings on fences, on porch railings, or spreading on their own over backyard vegetation.

Kadis shares her understanding of the complex dynamics

involved in conquests by invasive plants: "You have to use the word 'Oriental' with bittersweet, because there still is some American bittersweet in Massachusetts. A native species once present within the entire state from the Berkshires to Nantucket, American bittersweet is now almost entirely gone, state-listed as 'threatened'—likely due to invasion of Oriental bittersweet. The latter must have engulfed and 'dissolved' the native species by way of crossing with it and producing back-crosses over many years (that is, the hybrid progeny crossing again and again with the alien species, each generation thus inheriting less and less of the native genes). The same must have happened to the native phragmites and a few other native plants. This kind of threat from invasive species is even scarier than the mechanical displacement of natives!"[2]

Once one learns to recognize these invasive plants, they seem to be everywhere. Biking along the Cape Cod Canal, one sees spotted knapweed thriving along the path, even sprouting out of cracks in the pavement. Five years ago it could be found only at the eastern end of the canal's seven-mile length. Japanese knotweed is flourishing along the Phoenix Rail Trail on Massachusetts's South Coast, its rhizome or underground stem crossing under the paved surface to emerge on the other side. The shoots of phragmites penetrate straight up through the asphalt surface of Ellisville Road where it runs along the marsh edge.

These invasive plants are determined to spread from the roadside into pristine habitat. They establish themselves wherever their seeds happen to fall, and it does not take long for them to colonize new areas—they grow very rapidly. Once they take hold, they can alter key features of the landscape so dramatically that its ability to resist erosion, provide wildlife habitat, and retain plant diversity can be lost. Many parts of North America are experiencing an onslaught of these invaders, and few people are aware of it.

In the Back Marsh

One villain present at Ellisville Marsh is the common reed, typically referred to as phragmites, short for its scientific name *Phragmites australis*. Phragmites is a subaquatic grass. The plant grows as high as sixteen feet along the marsh edge in areas where the water is stagnant and poorly aerated. The least of the problems it creates in Ellisville Marsh is blocking the idyllic view of the salt marsh that used to be enjoyed by motorists passing by on Ellisville Road.

In addition to the edge of Ellisville Road, this plant can be found in the stagnant pool below the bluff on Lookout Point where the tidal inlet channel ran until late 2003. An additional stand of phragmites at the marsh's edge below the parking lot at Ellisville Harbor State Park was treated with herbicides by the Department of Conservation and Recreation (DCR) in late summer 2008. Scientific studies have shown that improving tidal flows to a salt marsh, as the Friends' inlet maintenance project was designed to do, should help control the spread of this plant naturally.

Phragmites likes brackish water and is hardy enough to survive in a wide range of wetland conditions, even on dry land. Its rhizomes can reach down six or more feet in the soil for water. The invasive subspecies of phragmites (the benign, native subspecies has virtually disappeared) is of great concern in salt marshes and other water bodies as it is often the first to arrive when the water in wetland areas stagnates and water quality becomes degraded. It spreads quickly and aggressively competes against native species for water and nutrients.

The plant releases toxins from its roots into the soil to kill surrounding plants in its vicinity.[3] Also like knapweed, phragmites displaces higher-quality plants in the ecosystem in a way that reduces plant diversity. It grows in dense colonies with as many as one hundred shoots per square meter, a density impenetrable for most wildlife, although it is ideally suited for the nests of marsh wrens, which are suspended like hammocks from its tall stalks.

Controlling the spread of phragmites is difficult because most nonchemical approaches, like cutting or pulling, not only result in rapid regrowth but also pose a risk of spreading the seeds. Improved tidal flow to the back marsh in Ellisville is expected to help. It is too early to tell whether it has.

Ironically, one recent scientific study suggests phragmites may actually play a beneficial role in a world facing a historic rise in sea level. This research suggested that phragmites may play a role similar to that of marsh cordgrass in providing food, protection, and habitat to estuarine and salt marsh inhabitants. Indeed, as Kadis is quick to point out, there are contradictory views among professionals when it comes to invasive plants.[4] One Massachusetts agency used to recommend beach rose for dune sand fixation; however, that position was later withdrawn. At least one restoration project in the Boston Harbor included the intentional planting of nonnative and invasive species.

In the Dunes and on the Beach

Without Kadis's practiced eye, the Friends might never have learned that spotted knapweed was a growing problem. She had found vast, well-maintained fields in nearby Myles Standish State Forest where the plant was in full bloom. Rapid spread is virtually guaranteed in the right environment. A single spotted knapweed plant can produce four hundred seeds.

It was Kadis's work at the state forest in 2011 that led the Friends to ask for her help at Ellisville Marsh. During her walk-around survey, she discovered significant colonies of spotted knapweed at both Ellisville Harbor State Park and Shifting Lots Preserve. It was displacing dune grass and other plant species to such an extent that the effect could be seen in aerial photographs. From above, the grassy dunes appeared to be going bald.

Spotted knapweed is native to Eastern Europe. There the plant is kept in check by knapweed root weevil and other weevils whose larvae and adults specialize in eating spotted knapweed. However, when the plant made it to North America, the weevil unfortunately remained at home. Spotted knapweed began to spread unabated.

According to the Minnesota Department of Agriculture, spotted knapweed was introduced to western Canada in the 1890s as a contaminant in agricultural seed and soil discarded from ship ballast. Since then the plant has become a chronic problem in pastures and rangeland throughout the western United States, devastating millions of acres.[5] It is spreading throughout the Northeast.

Spotted knapweed, like phragmites, has an ingenious way of clearing space for itself—its roots excrete a toxic chemical that kills neighboring plants and remains in the soil afterward. In fact, one pair of university researchers found that the toxin killed every plant they exposed to it.[6]

Kadis had learned that knapweed root weevil could be used as a form of biocontrol against the burgeoning colonies of spotted knapweed and that containers of the weevils could be obtained at relatively low cost from a supplier in Minnesota. No follow-up treatment is required. It sounded as simple as treating a grub-infested lawn with predatory nematodes, those helpful little worms that eat underground grub larvae. The adult weevils consume knapweed foliage; larvae hatch, burrow into the knapweed roots, and begin to eat, diminishing the ability of the invasive plants to develop.

There was a hitch. The place where the insect population had the best chance to establish itself and survive—the largest and densest infestation of spotted knapweed locally—was on the Ellisville Harbor State Park property. A permit would need to be obtained before the insects could be tested there however. Early feedback from DCR suggested that gaining this permission would involve a long, drawn-out process probably lasting months. Timing was critical. So a backup plan was devised.

A Friends member obtained a container of the insects and released the tiny predators on a private beachfront property test patch where the knapweed was in the early stages of establishing itself amid the dune grass. In a brief ceremony, the bugs were exhorted to venture as far as the eye could see in hopes of finding mother lodes of their favorite food. And off they went. They cannot fly so their impact is localized.

Unfortunately, there was no easy way to track the progress of this modest experiment. Visual inspection of the test site several years after release of the insects suggests there is less spotted knapweed present. Nevertheless, firing a salvo directly at the dense field of purple on the state park land would have provided a better opportunity for these hungry little herbivores to become established. One can only do so much with limited resources and time however. And the Friends' main mission is the restoration of tidal flows to a threatened salt marsh, not control of invasive plants. At least not yet.

Along the Road

Another hostile invader, Japanese knotweed, has taken over a good part of the dry land along the western perimeter of the salt marsh and is spreading vigorously. Ironically, the plant has begun to compete with phragmites along the marsh edge. Knotweed rhizomes have crossed under Ellisville Road and now make an attractive bordering feature for one of the homes there. And off it goes up the road, just like the spotted knapweed spreading along the Cape Cod Canal.

When a town road maintenance crew came by several years ago with a brush cutter to knock down the knotweed along the marsh edge and thereby improve the view, it grew back even denser. In fact, both knapweed and knotweed recover very nicely after being leveled. It turns out that it matters greatly how high up on the stalks one cuts the plant off.

Dr. Doug Johnson, a pulmonologist by day, has tackled the ambitious goal of eradicating Japanese knotweed in the Adirondacks and helped create a regional invasive plant control program focused on the plant. He can attest to its stubbornness and resilience. Johnson puts it simply: "For knotweed control, do not cut, dig, or mow," as tiny root or stem fragments can start new plants. Killing it takes direct injection of a herbicide called glyphosate into individual stems of the plant or spraying plants too small to inject.[7]

Treatments must be done when plants are taking nutrients to their rhizomes (e.g., August, September), and for large sites, several years of treatments may be needed for eradication. The DCR once retained a contractor to inject the stems of phragmites on its Ellisville Harbor State Park property. Within a few years, however, the stand had more or less fully recovered and begun spreading again.

These invasive plants are not only determined but tough. Their struggle with native plants might cause us to reflect on what it is about nature that allows species that seek to dominate all others to gain the upper hand so easily. To the Friends at least, it became apparent that newcomer plants fight dirty. Indigenous plants almost seem to be pacifists, yielding to the invaders too readily. Watching them battle for superiority at Ellisville Marsh is, sad to say, easy for humans to relate to.

But Kadis counters that plants must be judged innocent: "Every invasive species is native somewhere, and it is harmless wherever it belongs. Our native saltwater cordgrass has proved to be invasive when it was introduced to the Pacific Coast. More than that, it produced a monstrous hybrid with their native California cordgrass, so that now there is a real and uncontrollable problem. Quite a few of our native species are now listed as invasive in Europe. When I told a Russian botanist from Vladivostok that their Castor aralia (*Kalopanax septemlobus* = *K. pictus*) is a new invasive tree here, she refused to believe me, as for her this is a rare, state-protected species. The only truly invasive species on the planet is us. If it were not for people moving plants and animals around the globe, there would not be the phenomenon of invasive species."[8]

What key lessons have we learned by watching plants in and around Ellisville Marsh? That there is richness and diversity in this ecosystem beyond the typical limits of our imagination, and that the flora is continuously developing in new directions.

Learning about the plant life at Ellisville Marsh brings key questions to the fore. What version of a natural state should we try and restore to? How should the fact that we ourselves have accelerated the evolution of the ecosystem by introducing invasive species influence decision-making? Perhaps the Friends' preference for the word "revitalize," rather than "restore," is more apropos than the organization's founders knew.

As Ellen Russell points out, there is a broader context for thinking about vegetation at Ellisville Marsh:

> The vegetation in Ellisville Marsh consists of relatively few species—fourteen to be exact—in comparison to the abundance of flora that inhabits the edges of the marsh .... Only a few species can withstand regular diurnal submergence with the high pH and high salt environment that the ocean provides through very unique physiologic adaptations. These particular plants, of which *Spartina alterniflora* and *Spartina patens* are the two most abundant in Ellisville Marsh, have been monitored ... using a network of fixed vegetation plots. ...
>
> In general, *S. alterniflora* across the marsh has stayed fairly constant throughout the years—gaining in some areas and declining in others. *S. patens* has experienced a general decline in this marsh, and in marshes across the Cape as well. Areas of bare [mudflats] and wrack [organic matter such as seaweed, kelp, shells, and other debris deposited at high tide] have increased. It is unclear how

many factors other than tidal hydrology contribute to these changes; however, extreme storms and other weather-er patterns associated with long-term climate change are expected to be among them.

What does this mean for the health of the marsh? While the marsh system is a complicated and delicately balanced one, it also has amazing resilience. For example, more bare area translates to more foraging ground for birds. More wrack means more organic matter to increase the elevation of the marsh. As far as the vegetation is concerned, these primary producers will be in a constant state of flux given increasing tidal range and the counter-acting forces of marsh building through sand and wrack deposition. We continue to monitor these changes with the hope of guiding any long-term solutions for channel maintenance toward one that offers the greatest benefit to the marsh ecosystem.[9]

The quiet battle between indigenous and nonnative plant species continues at Ellisville Marsh, reshaping the coastal landscape little by little.

CHAPTER 4

The Crux of the Problem

NATURE'S PERFECT MOSAIC OF plants and wildlife is on full display at Ellisville Marsh, yet it is impacted by seemingly random events. The fearsome energy released by a winter nor'easter or the drop of a tiny seed from a bird's grasp can disrupt the natural order and create chaos. Change comes in small ways or large, slowly or in an instant. And in nature, change always carries consequences. Ellisville Marsh is itself a consequence of a great historical event—the Ice Age.

Ellisville Marsh was molded by glaciers. During their advance and retreat in distant times, glaciers carved their way through southeastern Massachusetts and left behind piles of boulders, small hills known as glacial moraines, kettle holes and ponds, streambeds, and valleys. One can see the scars the glaciers left behind when walking on forest trails or standing on the coastal bluff overlooking the ocean. Glaciers sculpted the shorelines, accentuated the bluffs, scoured coves and inlets.

Estuaries formed where rivers and streams followed valleys to the sea. Sand spits settled into place along the coastline and lengthened over time, creating lagoons and salt marshes in their shadow. In the millennia since, such natural reengineering has never surrendered its constancy. Coastal erosion reshapes the landscape the glaciers wrought. Sand is continuously flowing along the coastline, drawn from some beaches and filling nooks, crannies, and inlets in others. The coastal landscape changes on a daily basis.

Drifting sand is a continuous, natural reality. Sand becomes fluid, suspended in the seawater. Engineered structures have little hope of halting its movement. We have not always understood well enough how the sand moves to avoid the unintended consequences of our often-clumsy interventions. Attempts to stop sand migration invariably produce consequences. And as the sand moves, so does the Ellisville Marsh inlet.

Historical records and drawings suggest that the Ellisville Marsh inlet has been peripatetic for hundreds, likely thousands of years. Hand-drawn maps from 1794 and 1830 show the marsh inlet a half mile north of its present location. A sketch map from 1872 places it a few hundred yards south of its present position. Another from eighteen years later, in Ellis's *Reminiscences*, suggests the inlet had shifted back north, to a place near the northern tip of what is now Ellisville Harbor State Park.[1] The inlet was abruptly moved to its present location, historical records suggest, by an event that occurred on the cusp of the twentieth century.

An Era of Superstorms

The blizzard known as the Portland Gale struck the coast of New England with extreme malevolence in November 1898. This ferocious storm formed when two low-pressure areas came together off the coast of Virginia and moved up the coast, producing hurricane-force winds on Nantucket Sound and a storm surge as high as ten feet in normally placid Cohasset Harbor, just south of Boston.[2]

Unaware of the monster bearing down on New England, the SS *Portland* departed Boston for Portland, Maine, on its scheduled run November 27. It never arrived. The steamship sank in the storm, and none of her 192 passengers and crew survived.

In all, some 150 vessels were lost that week in the region's worst maritime tragedy of the nineteenth century.

Beyond the tragic loss of life and ships, the Portland Gale inflicted epic damage on the New England coastline. Among the storm's lesser-known impacts, the Ellisville Marsh inlet shifted a half mile south to its present location.

Subsequent storms included Hurricane Bob in August 1991, the Perfect Storm a few months later, the Storm of the Century in 1993, and Superstorm Sandy in 2012. Each storm caused lasting damage to the coastal bank, barrier beaches, and inlets throughout the Gulf of Maine, especially on outer Cape Cod, where the coastal land form itself is a fabric woven by threads of sand shifting inexorably over time.[3]

Such storms are classified by the National Oceanic and Atmospheric Administration as "extreme storms." In this era of climate change and sea level rise, it is expected that such storms will become more frequent visitors to our shores. We must understand their direct effects and indirect consequences if we are to have any hope of mitigating their impacts.

The spectacle of a winter nor'easter rolling in, its angry surf crashing into the rock jetty at Ellisville, is something to behold. The forces in play are at once fearsome and awe inspiring. Waves elevated to ten or twelve feet by prolonged, near-hurricane-force winds slam into the boulders, exploding into white clouds of spray that can be seen from a distance. The jetty itself takes on the appearance of a ship plowing through open seas. As the storm-driven surf mounts its fullest assault, water cascades over the jetty and takes a roller-coaster ride into the channel. A column of suspended sand colors the seawater a dingy yellow.

At high tide the jetty itself is fully submerged and disappears into the maelstrom. Once the storm has spent its fury and the tide retreats, what lies below the waves gradually reappears, exposing a changed landscape. A large tongue of sand called a "barrier spit" has been formed by the great plug of sand the storm has washed over the jetty.

A Barrier Spit Forms

The barrier spit formed by a major storm can easily be six to eight feet high and as long as a thousand feet. It is the seed from which a higher and longer sandbar grows, showing itself above the waterline during most hours of successive tide cycles. It adds mass over time until it becomes a strip of dry land bridging southward from Ellisville Harbor State Park into Shifting Lots Preserve. The straight channel path is blocked by its presence and bends southward. A new cycle of inlet blockage has been triggered.

Over the course of a few hours of a storm, nature can move a volume of sand as great as ten thousand cubic yards, three times the amount regulatory permits allow the Friends to excavate when periodic inlet maintenance is performed. Nature requires no permits.

To the best of our knowledge, none of those who hold sway over the Friends' regulatory permits have ever witnessed firsthand the intense drama that produces a new barrier spit at the Ellisville Marsh inlet. To see a storm at its height of power and ferocity is to understand in an instant how the barrier spit comes into being and to know that nothing we undertake to stop it will fully succeed. It is only a matter of time before nature will overpower whatever we put in its way. The Friends' 2013 annual report provided a snapshot of the increasing storm threat to the salt marsh inlet:

> A succession of major coastal storms hit Massachusetts over the winter, causing barrier beach erosion of historic proportions. Ellisville was no exception. First came Superstorm Sandy, which hit on Monday, October 29, with its hurricane force winds and heavy surf. Only a week later, a powerful nor'easter rolled in on Election Day. The latter storm hit Ellisville with more raw violence than Sandy and formed a new barrier spit that partially blocked the Ellisville inlet and began restricting tidal flows into and out of the marsh.

The Friends reopened the blocked inlet in early January only to have the Blizzard of 2013 (Nemo) block it again in February. Under a permit modification we requested from the MassDEP and enabled by an emergency grant, we again reopened the inlet in early March. Whether this storm pattern was a harbinger of climate change or not, the experience made it clear that we need to explore alternative ways, both regulatory and physical, to ensure that the inlet remains open.[4]

Storms do not tell the whole story though. Coastal evolution and inlet migration occur imperceptibly across the minutes, hours, and days. Sand drifts southward along the east-facing coastline at Ellisville. Unlike the juvenile fish that swim here and there in the shallows, sand only goes where the water takes it. Coastal geomorphologists, scientists who study the evolution of the coastline as it is influenced by winds, waves, currents, and tides, refer to this mechanism as "sediment transport" or "littoral drift." A river of sand runs along the coastline. The process accelerates during winter when strong northeasterly winds prevail and the most powerful coastal storms develop.

The Problem with Coastal Structures

With a fetch of twenty-five miles across Cape Cod Bay, prevailing winter northeasterlies drive waves in a direction that carries sand southward along the Massachusetts coast, shifting sandbars and piling sand next to coastal structures such as rock groins and jetties. Many of these structures were built in the sixties to trap sand and preserve sandy beaches.

It is now widely understood that placing hardened structures on the coastline produces unintended consequences. Downdrift beaches become starved of sand and lose their natural resistance to erosion. The wearing down and, in some places, collapse of the coastal bank accelerates. Sand drifting along the coastline interferes with the timeless, natural process of sediment transport and creates winners and losers. Some beaches gain sand, others give it up.

The 1960 rock jetty that helps define the north side of the Ellisville Marsh inlet is one such barrier to the movement of sediment. It was designed to catch sand. The jetty, a linear arrangement of boulders carefully fitted together and running perpendicular to the shoreline, extends from the grass dune into the bay, its seaward end standing in a few feet of water even at dead low tide. The structure, now mostly in ruins after sixty years of battering by constant wave action and periodic storms, has complicated the challenge of keeping the marsh inlet open and tidal flows unrestricted.

Built by a Massachusetts state agency, the rock jetty successfully blocked sand from migrating south and into the inlet for a decade after it was constructed, according to Ellisville old-timers. A height of perhaps ten feet of sand was captured on the jetty's north side and held back from reaching the inlet. And there the sand remained stockpiled for years.

The problem arises with powerful winter nor'easters. The large waves they generate overwash the jetty and carry thousands of cubic yards of the stockpiled sand into the salt marsh channel all at once. The volume of material coming over the jetty during a major storm can be so massive that the outgoing flow through the channel—more than a hundred thousand gallons per minute on average—is unable to flush it out into the bay. Limits exist as to how much material can be scoured by tidal action, even when the water is tightly channeled through a narrow opening, pressurized like a fire hose.

The technical term for closure of a salt marsh inlet by sand is "avulsion," which means abandonment or relocation of a channel. Avulsion is a common occurrence in salt marshes and river deltas around the world. A sand barrier spit forms perpendicular to the channel, forcing the flow to take a sharp turn when it reaches the spit (the "bent hose" effect). This begins a gradual process of spit elongation.

Once even a small barrier spit has formed, subsequent tide cycles pile sand on it, adding to its height and length. This further diverts the inlet and lengthens the path through which the tidal water must course. For the Ellisville Marsh inlet, the combination of a hardened rock jetty with its stored-up, ever-ready supply of sand and superstorms periodically overwashing the structure constitutes a direct threat to the inlet and the tidal flows it enables. A tidal inlet that is even partially blocked can negatively impact the marsh's health.

Seawater floods a salt marsh when the tide comes in. The marsh drains as the tide recedes. Tidal exchange is as important to a salt marsh as breathing is for humans. Any blockage must be removed so tidal flows can come and go unobstructed. Beginning with the 1991 hurricane, formation of the barrier spit and its accompanying blockage of the Ellisville Marsh inlet became a routine occurrence. The blockage became a long-term concern as local residents could no longer remove it as the lobstermen once did.

Death of a Salt Marsh

Does keeping the Ellisville Marsh inlet open contribute to the health of plants, fish, and wildlife in the salt marsh? Most scientists think so. Friends members ardently believe so. However, when one sets out to tackle an environmental problem, whether it involves reopening a blocked salt marsh inlet or intervening to protect a Piping Plover nest from predators, one looks to science.

We older generations were taught in school that science holds the answers. We came to have faith that science can explain the inner workings of a complex ecosystem. We trust that science can tell us what to do and how best to do it. Whether or not everyone believes in science is, these days at least, another matter.

But what happens when scientific opinions conflict with knowledge borne of long human experience? Scientific opinions almost always trump deep experience when it comes to environmental permitting. Ask a staff person at a Massachusetts environmental agency who they are more inclined to believe: a geo-coastal engineer who creates computer simulation models of the coastal system or generations of farmers and fishermen who watched the tides come and go for a hundred years and whose insights have been passed down.

The project at Ellisville Marsh encapsulates this tension. Old-timers or modern-day scientists? On whose knowledge should decisions about environmental restoration be based? Is it right to discount the observations of people who have lived in an intimate relationship with a natural place for hundreds of years in favor of scientists who might depend on computer models to explain physical changes?

If we depend more heavily on scientific input, can the science tell us everything we need to know about the underlying mechanisms that contribute to a healthy salt marsh? Can we hope to capture every important factor, natural and unnatural (a fitting adjective for man's periodic and sometimes ill-advised interventions), to fully explain why a salt marsh ecosystem behaves as it does?

Indicators exist that explain much about the health of a salt marsh. Certain wetland plants are very picky about their environment and can thus tell us much about natural conditions. As previously noted, *Spartina alterniflora* is a key species that indicates the health of New England coastal marshes. People involved with salt marsh restoration tend to refer to the plant by its scientific name or a shortened version of the name, *S. alterniflora*.

S. alterniflora is important to consider because it thrives only in a narrow range of water levels and salinity conditions. So when the salt marsh's tidal inlet becomes blocked and tidal flows are restricted, the salt marsh begins to die. *S. alterniflora* is often the first to go. If the plant is dying off, something is out of kilter.

Extensive die-off of wetlands vegetation, especially *S. alterniflora*, occurred in Ellisville Marsh after the marsh inlet became blocked in late 1991. In particular, the low marsh became increasingly waterlogged, and high-value plants were unable to tolerate the new conditions and became stressed.

One might quite reasonably ask why a salt marsh cannot simply function as a salt pond when its inlet to the sea becomes blocked and tidal flows are diminished. Why does a salt marsh ecosystem require twice-daily flushing with saltwater? The answer is that the unique communities of plants that live in a salt marsh environment have evolved over millions of years to a state in which their survival depends on a certain level of salinity and a certain cycle of being submerged and exposed to the air, the so-called tidal range. These plants are sensitive to even slight changes in environmental conditions.

A natural environment would no doubt exist, and might be quite healthy, if the marsh inlet were to close entirely. The pre-existing, natural system would simply no longer function as a salt marsh or estuary. Moreover, it could take decades for the transition from salt marsh to salt pond or freshwater pond to be completed, a period in which species that critically depend on salt marsh conditions would be unable to survive. It is likely that invasive plant species such as phragmites would rapidly expand their coverage within the marsh as conditions deteriorated and water quality became degraded.

Salt marsh die-off is a phenomenon that has been observed across the United States and Europe for decades. Large swaths of S. alterniflora suddenly begin to die, leaving bare mudflats in their place. Why is this so alarming? Because salt marshes are a critical wetland resource. Anything that compromises their health and vitality is a concern. Saltmarsh cordgrass in particular holds sediment in place and helps preserve vital wetlands habitat. When the cordgrass dies, erosion accelerates and mudbanks collapse into the creeks that crisscross the marsh.

Shortly before the Friends organization was formed in 2007, articles about salt marsh die-off began appearing in Cape Cod newspapers and the *Boston Globe*.[5] Ellisville Marsh was among the salt marshes where the phenomenon was keenly observed.

One 2015 article noted that from 1984 to 2013, five of six salt marshes studied lost between 24 and 48 percent of their coverage of the high marsh grass that characterizes a healthy salt marsh. The study goes on to say that these losses are primarily because of sea level rise, which was estimated to be 6.3 inches over the same period. The sixth site lost 92 percent—much of it due to physical changes. The article highlighted expert views on the value of salt marsh habitat on Cape Cod: "They aren't just dying—they are disappearing, according to a new study by Cape Cod National Seashore plant ecologist Stephen Smith, which demonstrates that sea level rise is outpacing the natural capacity of sea marshes to adjust. 'The endgame could be extensive mudflats, home to snails, or, if the water quality is good enough, sea grass. Although snails, worms, and mollusks use mudflats and fish and shellfish species inhabit sea grass ecosystems (such as eel grass), there is nowhere near the variety and abundance of life exhibited in salt marshes,'" Smith said.[6]

One of the specific methods to slow the loss of salt marsh habitat cited in the article is to improve the connection of the salt marsh with the ocean. This is what the Friends' inlet maintenance work strives to do. However, it is typically undersized culverts that restrict tidal flows on the Cape. This contrasts with the natural process of avulsion that occurs at the Ellisville inlet.

A state-sponsored study of salt marsh die-off completed just a few months before formation of the Friends in 2007 listed Ellisville Marsh as being one of the most severely impacted of salt marsh sites surveyed, stating, "The effects on the Ellisville Harbor site on the South Shore are likely linked to the periodic shift in salinity due to natural coastal sedimentation and periodic opening and closing of the mouth to tidal flow. The dramatic changes in salinity may have significantly altered marsh vegetation on a periodic basis."[7]

Tidal range, that is, how high the water rises and how completely it drains with each tide cycle, is a major factor influencing *S. alterniflora* health in the salt marsh. As has been noted, salt-marsh cordgrass cannot tolerate being submerged for too long.

The plant literally begins to drown when a blocked inlet makes it impossible for the water to drain out of the marsh properly.

Tidal flow restriction, which is closely related to changing salinity, was identified in the 2007 study as a major factor influencing the health of Ellisville Marsh. Periodic blockage of the inlet appeared to be the main culprit behind salt marsh die-off, although there are differing opinions about the precise mechanism by which this occurs.

William Hubbard, who at the time of his visit to Ellisville Marsh in 2001 was chief of the Environmental Resources Branch of the US Army Corps of Engineers, observed, "It seems from the site visit that your wetlands are drowning and are experiencing a drastic salinity change due to tidal restrictions."[8] After surveying conditions in Ellisville Marsh from his kayak a year later, Ed Reiner, a senior wetland scientist with the US Environmental Protection Agency, echoed Hubbard's assertion, stating, "I believe that the die-off of salt marsh vegetation is attributable to changes in the tidal hydrology since the former channel closed off and the new channel formed."[9] Reiner would remain interested in the project for the next twenty years. He was one of the only local, state, or federal officials who went out of their way to periodically visit the marsh for a firsthand look at its condition.

The Role of Science

Scientific investigation offers insights into the condition of the salt marsh ecosystem and the effects of periodic and prolonged inlet closure. Ellisville Marsh itself has been the focus of several scientific papers related to inlet migration, tidal flow resistance, and wetlands response to a diminished tidal range.

The scientific paper most directly and closely related to the Friends' mission of revitalizing Ellisville Marsh is Ellen Russell's 2019 doctoral thesis entitled "Factors Influencing *Spartina alterniflora* Productivity in Relationship to Estuary Inlet Reopening, Ellisville Marsh, Plymouth, MA."[10] To ensure her scientific independence, Russell resigned from the Friends' board of directors while she pursued her research.

Russell's project involved a pre-dredge versus post-dredge statistical analysis of twenty-seven interdependent chemical, biological, and physical variables, such as soil within one-meter-square plots. Variables included stem density counts and percent coverage estimates for vegetation, data that Friends volunteers have collected for more than a decade. Russell applied statistical tests to determine if these variables were significantly different before and after the inlet was dredged.

Russell also performed detailed analyses of the tidal range in Ellisville Marsh and found that it significantly improved in 2011 and 2012, compared with pre-dredge conditions in 2010. Her data, collected using barometric pressure loggers placed in test locations over a period of several years, indicated that mean tidal range in the marsh increased by approximately 200 millimeters after the summer of 2010. Increasing the tidal range was the Friends' primary objective when the organization pursued regulatory permits to reopen the blocked Ellisville inlet.

Russell's thesis project confirmed that reopening the blocked tidal inlet resulted in a widened tidal range (the marsh filled and drained more completely). Geographic information system (GIS) analysis of aerial and on-the-ground estimates of percentage coverage by vegetation showed increases in *S. alterniflora*, prevalent in the low-marsh areas, and decreases in saltmeadow cordgrass (also known as *Spartina patens* or *S. patens*) over time. Ellisville Marsh is made up more of low marsh than high.

Even nonscientists will be impressed by the lengths to which Russell went to understand how intervention by the Friends impacted plant health. She examined stem densities, below-ground biomass, water chemistry, and even the extent to which inlet reopening impacted certain insect pests in the marsh. All of her findings were backed up by several years of laboriously crawling around in the marsh on summer days, many of which were excessively hot and humid.

Throughout the marsh, she set out nearly one hundred sampling plots in parallel lines or transects.[11] Each plot is located by a PVC marker pipe jammed deeply into the marsh bottom and measures one meter by one meter. Each summer during the study, either Russell or a Friends environmental intern laboriously estimated the percentage coverage of saltmarsh cordgrass and other plant species within the plot area. Some years, the salt marsh inlet was blocked; in others, it was open.

The project was thorough and conducted with scientific independence. Russell determined that reopening the blocked Ellisville Marsh inlet was a net-positive intervention. However, in her thesis she suggests that any claims regarding the specific benefits of maintaining the inlet to widen tidal range must be appropriately nuanced.

An earlier scientific paper was written in 2006 by Vlad Hruby's consultant, geo-coastal engineer John Ramsey of Applied Coastal Research and Engineering, and several coauthors from the School of Marine Science and Technology at the University of Massachusetts–Dartmouth. Their paper, "Quantifying the Influence of Inlet Migration on Tidal Marsh System Health," also specifically considered Ellisville Marsh and sought to describe the specific impact of the reopening of the marsh inlet by Vlad Hruby in late 2003 after it had been partially closed for more than a decade.[12]

Like Russell, Ramsey and his coauthors looked at pre- and post-dredge conditions in the marsh and determined that tidal range in the marsh increased measurably as a result of the inlet reopening. The Ramsey study, however, concluded that *S. alterniflora* responded to the improved tidal exchange by rebounding quickly, expanding its coverage area by a remarkable 170 percent within a few short years.

Some of the favorable findings in Ramsey's paper on the Ellisville inlet reopening came under direct attack from staff persons at one Massachusetts environmental agency. In fact, disagreements over fundamental scientific issues surfaced at several of the Friends' permitting meetings. Representatives of the Friends in attendance witnessed "dueling banjos," scientific-style. Public officials openly challenged the validity of Ramsey's findings.

The Friends acknowledge that positive statements in the Ramsey paper about the quick rebound of wetlands plants after the 2003 inlet reopening are likely to have favorably influenced permitting work to reopen and maintain the Ellisville Marsh inlet. However, the organization's board considers his finding of rapid recolonization of *S. alterniflora* to be unsupported by available scientific evidence. The important point here, though, is that Russell and Ramsey agreed that maintaining the inlet helps preserve an adequate tidal range and promotes the health of wetland vegetation such as *S. alterniflora*. The salt marsh is better off when the inlet is open and tidal flows are unrestricted, according to both research studies.

What do scientific studies gain us in terms of building consensus about appropriate actions to take when complex ecosystems like salt marshes are threatened? Sadly, the answer based on the Friends' experience is, Not enough. This is not to say that scientific research is of little value to our level of understanding. The problem lies with entrenched bureaucracies, varying scientific methodologies, and, sometimes, personal or professional self-interest. These dynamics can undermine the well-intentioned efforts of environmental stewards whose decisions and plans depend on the role that sound and reliable science must play.

There are practical questions as well. Is it better to maintain the inlet minimally on an annual basis, as the fishermen used to do, or to do so only when scientific models tell us the length of the barrier spit has passed a tipping point at which direct harm is likely to be inflicted on the salt marsh ecosystem? For Ellisville Marsh, the Ramsey paper suggests that a barrier spit longer than 190 meters will cause some ecological harm to the salt marsh, the level of which increases significantly when the spit extends past 310 meters.

Notwithstanding what can or cannot be concluded from the data, one thing is clear. The recent level of scientific scrutiny and fieldwork at this salt marsh and its barrier beach exceeds anything the Commonwealth of Massachusetts undertook after 1960 when the decision was made to construct the rock jetty, the structure that has proved to be so problematic. The wide-ranging environmental monitoring and data collection programs conducted by Friends volunteers for more than fifteen years have made Ellisville Marsh one of the most closely studied salt marshes in Massachusetts, perhaps *the* most studied.

There is general scientific consensus that keeping the Ellisville Marsh inlet open to maintain tidal flows is vital for healthy marsh vegetation and water quality. When the inlet becomes blocked, the health of the marsh suffers and key native plant species begin to die. However, the question of how best to go about maintaining the inlet over time has not yet been fully answered in the context of sea level rise and increasingly intense storms. The Friends organization believes there is value in listening to the old-timers. The fishermen and the farmers, and the Indigenous people long before them, deeply understood how nature works in this special place. They knew how to listen for the marsh's heartbeat. They were connected to nature.

CHAPTER 5
....
Birth of a Backyard Movement

⌐

MEMBERS OF TODAY'S ELLISVILLE community have become more closely connected to Ellisville Marsh, largely as the result of a regulatory enforcement action. The Massachusetts Department of Environmental Protection (MassDEP) consent order in its 2005 case against Ellisville resident Vlad Hruby required him to form a nonprofit to avoid a recurrence of what it saw as unauthorized work at the Ellisville Marsh inlet.[1]

It would have been difficult for Hruby to satisfy this requirement by himself. Neighbors stepped in to help, and the nonprofit Friends of Ellisville Marsh, Inc., was created. It became the organization that would pursue regulatory permits and assume responsibility for maintaining the Ellisville Marsh inlet as envisioned by the MassDEP. This all took place in mid-2007.

Although it had no paid staff and has not received taxpayer funding, the young nonprofit soon outstripped original expectations, widened its focus, and saw noteworthy accomplishments, some of which were unprecedented in Massachusetts. Yet, even after fifteen years, the Friends of Ellisville Marsh remains a work in progress. Its path forward is still tenuous, and its ultimate success is not assured, despite many thousands of hours of work by its volunteer board and membership.

How did the nonprofit come about? Five neighbors on a street called Lookout Point in Plymouth, taking a giant leap of faith, came together as the board of directors of the newly formed Friends of Ellisville Marsh, which the MassDEP's consent order had required. The five founding directors were Eric Cody, Bob Goldthwaite, Peter Hruby, Ellen Russell, and Jack Scambos, each discussed below. These founders could not have imagined the daunting scale of the task that lay before them. If they had, it is likely none would have volunteered. The level of effort and financial resources just to obtain the local, state, and federal permits needed to reopen and maintain the blocked salt marsh inlet would be significant. And accomplishing those preliminary steps would just make more work possible.

The new nonprofit would need to raise funds, conduct scientific studies, develop an ongoing communications program, track membership, and record revenues and expenses for IRS and state reporting. None of the founders had heard of a Certificate for Solicitation or were aware that one was needed to operate a nonprofit in Massachusetts. Later on there would need to be construction oversight. Supervising a contractor tasked with excavating the blocked Ellisville Marsh inlet within the narrow confines of environmental regulations and permit conditions would be challenging.

Some of the founding directors grew up next to the salt marsh or spent summers there. Others wanted to address the problem of erosion of the coastal bank. Still others were midlife idealists driven by the possibility of doing something meaningful. None had previously been environmental permit holders. Would a variety of good intentions be enough? One precursor to the project existed, and its experience might best be described as cautionary.

The Impetus for the Project

Five years earlier, Vlad Hruby had retained Applied Coastal Research and Engineering, a consulting firm on Cape Cod, to advise him on how to protect his property on Lookout Point Road from continuing erosion caused by the migrating Ellisville

Marsh inlet. His home, a one-story cottage the family used on weekends and in the summer, was inching closer to the edge of the coastal bank on which it sat with every passing season. Major storms sped up the process, sometimes taking a bite of several feet from his home's frontage overlooking the sea.

In Hruby's case, a natural dynamic was at play: the Ellisville Marsh inlet had become blocked, and the salt marsh channel had migrated some fifteen hundred feet south along the beach, at which point it hit a rock groin standing in its way. Unable to continue migrating southward, the channel was redirected sharply to the east and out into the bay. Seen from above, the overall path the water took as it left the marsh and made its way to the sea resembled a large Z.

At the channel's final hook to the east, the water flowing into the curve had carved out a niche in the coastal bank the Hruby house sat on, eating into the bluff and undermining it at the bottom. The damage traveled up the slope as sand and vegetation above the scar gradually collapsed over time. Had the problem been left unaddressed, the house might have fallen over within a decade. That a migrating salt marsh inlet would directly threaten their home was not something the Hrubys had remotely considered when they bought the cottage a decade earlier.

John Ramsey, the geo-coastal engineer who would later coauthor the scientific paper mentioned above, advised Hruby that unless the marsh inlet was restored to its historical location, the channel would likely continue to cause erosion damage to the bluff. He recommended that Hruby urgently pursue the regulatory permits that would allow a one-time, emergency reopening of the blocked inlet. Restoring the channel to its straight east-west layout would take the pressure off the coastal bank.

A year later, after having spent a considerable amount of money on surveyors, consultants, and application fees, Hruby had his permits in hand. Fifteen more feet of Hruby's front yard had collapsed in the interim. Excavators were brought to the site in late November 2003 to breach the barrier spit and bury several concrete "jersey barriers" in excavated sand to block the unwanted channel path heading south. The work was completed in several days, wrapping up just after Thanksgiving. But the project quickly hit a snag.

In a cruel twist, an early winter storm hit the area within days and reblocked the inlet—uncertainty is the nature of this game. But the equipment had not yet been removed from the site, and the regulatory window for site work was still technically open under Hruby's emergency permits. Taking advantage of this, the contractor reopened the inlet a second time. Seawater resumed flowing in and out of the marsh on a straight and direct path as it had for most of the preceding century. But nearly twenty years had passed since such an inlet profile had existed. It would take a decade or more for the salt marsh to reach a new, natural equilibrium.

Part of the 2003 work entailed constructing a berm or soft barrier along the south side of the channel with the excavated sand. This berm was to help hold the newly dug channel in place. The jersey barriers were buried in this barrier to block the old channel path and give it resistance to breaching while the inlet adjusted to its new profile over time. Other than the two parallel sets of jersey barriers that served as its backbone, the berm consisted entirely of sand and small cobble. The material itself provided no structural support to hold the berm, hence the channel, in place.

By 2005, the soft channel berm had been ground down by wave and tidal action, fully exposing the jersey barriers. The heavy reinforced-steel concrete barriers had been torqued badly out of position by the twice-daily force of the outgoing water flows. The Hruby family brought in a contractor with a small piece of equipment that year to put sand back and restore the berm. This was, at least in the eyes of some experienced in regulatory matters, not a big deal. But in Hruby's case, the 2005 touch-up work became a big deal.

A MassDEP Enforcement Action

The brouhaha that followed this brief work event began with a disgruntled kayaker. He had been driving his car to the edge of the former Ellisville harbor to launch his kayak until 2003, when the new beach management plan that went with the gift of land to the Wildlands Trust put an end to vehicular beach access. On seeing the 2005 berm repair work being performed, he filed a complaint with the MassDEP. In the agency's eyes, a one-time permit truly means one time. It may have been the case that Hruby was made an example of by the MassDEP to reassert its authority.

The MassDEP's view was that once Hruby had completed his work in late 2003, there was no authorization to do anything further. After an investigation, the MassDEP concluded that the permits had been overstepped and, more important, that no final water quality certification had been issued. The latter infraction, at least, appears to have been the result of poor communication between Hruby and Ramsey.

Once the agency had determined that a violation had occurred, negotiations over the penalty began between the MassDEP and Hruby's attorney, Don Quinn. Quinn was able to convince the MassDEP to reduce the monetary penalty from $10,000 to a symbolic $1,000, with the difference to be made up by volunteer hours in programs to improve the condition of the marsh.

The consent order, or settlement, in the MassDEP's case against Hruby contained an attachment, titled "Supplemental Environmental Project," that required him to establish a non-profit organization to be called the Friends of Ellisville Marsh, with the following, prespecified mission:

- Restore, preserve, and maintain the Ellisville Marsh ecosystem.

- Organize volunteer and consulting support for monitoring and scientific research studies.

- Undertake fundraising for the benefit of the Ellisville Marsh ecosystem.

- Hold regulatory permits for, and supervise mainte-nance of, the Ellisville Marsh channel, in compliance with all applicable regulatory requirements and permitting conditions.

- Facilitate discussions between the owner of the Shifting Lots Preserve, other related parties, and various federal, state, and local regulatory agencies, and prepare grant applications for scientific studies of the Ellisville Marsh ecosystem.[2]

This mission statement was drafted by Quinn to satisfy the MassDEP's need that something meaningful and positive result from the incident. It did much more, altering the course of events at Ellisville Marsh. The Friends of Ellisville Marsh, Inc., was cre-ated as a Massachusetts Chapter 180 nonprofit corporation to pursue the revitalization of this sensitive environmental resource. All five of the points in the MassDEP's consent order were cut and pasted into the nonprofit's articles of incorporation.

Created as the remedy for Hruby's alleged wrongdoing at the Ellisville inlet, the nonprofit was a case of lemons being turned into lemonade, thanks to Quinn's foresight. One has to wonder how many other nonprofits have had their mission statements specified in an order from an environmental protection agency. It was an unusual beginning for a project that was unlikely to suc-ceed given the long odds it faced. The organization's fate would ultimately depend on those who stepped up to meet the challenge.

A Crusade Is Launched

It is the character of individuals who undertake a challenge like the revitalization of Ellisville Marsh that often determines whether the venture will succeed or fail. How persistent are they? Do they shy away from barriers in the road ahead? Can they work together?

In hindsight, the Friends of Ellisville Marsh was fortunate. A group of committed people rallied to tackle the challenges. Little did any realize they were setting out on a journey with an unknown destination and an indefinite time frame. It turned out to be more than the start of a journey—it was to become a crusade.

Fifteen years of collaboration to revitalize Ellisville Marsh have created enduring friendships, uncovered a diverse set of perspectives, and promoted mutual understanding and goodwill. Looking back, it is hard to appreciate that some of the project's founders were barely acquainted when this undertaking began. All became friends and kindred spirits, allies with a shared purpose. Their enthusiasm for the work spread through the local community. Most developed a deeper, more personal connection with this special place. Some learned more about themselves than they did about the salt marsh.

There was a predecessor organization of sorts. The Lookout Point Improvement Association (LOPIA) existed because a neighborhood well at the end of Salt Marsh Lane used to supply water to houses up and down Lookout Point. In effect, LOPIA was a small, private water company. By 2003, however, municipal water had been extended to all the houses in the neighborhood, rendering LOPIA's water system obsolete.

Prior to the demise of the neighborhood water system, LOPIA had become the center of neighborhood discussions regarding the salt marsh. A group made up of a number of Ellisville families— Tom and Patty Russell (Ellen Russell's parents) and the Baileys, Lekbergs, Martinos, Marshes, Quinns, and Scamboses—had begun discussing how to protect Ellisville Marsh. In fact, thanks to efforts by Paul Martino, the US Army Corps of Engineers considered a project to reopen the Ellisville Marsh inlet in 2001. Then came 9/11. Momentum for the project was instantly, and permanently, lost.

Martino was LOPIA's president at the time. He was energetic and outgoing. He collected the minimal, annual dues and kept the neighborhood informed of developments. He and his wife, Bobbi, who later became one of the original members of the Friends' threatened species monitoring team, lived in a beautifully crafted home on Salt Marsh Lane with an angled view of the salt marsh. When the Martinos first visited Ellisville for a weekend in 1969, Bobbi felt a kinship with the place. It was no wonder. She was returning to her ancestral home, being a tenth-generation descendant of the settler John Ellis.

Paul Martino had a strong interest in the history of the salt marsh, measured by the number of hours he spent in the rare books and manuscripts room at the Plymouth Public Library perusing historical documents. He assembled a collection of excerpts from these records that made others aware that Ellisville Marsh was a place with an extensive history and rich, natural features worth preserving, a place worth fighting for. He hosted meetings with functionaries from state and federal agencies at the time Vlad Hruby set out to halt the erosion of the coastal bank in front of his house.

Martino chronicled the history of the inlet and documented past projects that had been undertaken by the state, creating a case history for the permitting of new inlet work as the successor to a previously established maintenance project. It undoubtedly helped that Martino, aided by his wife's gregarious nature, knew virtually everyone in the neighborhood, including Al Marsh.

For more than twenty years, Martino had tried to unify the neighborhood behind actions to reverse the environmental damage and improve oversight at Ellisville Marsh. However, as a retired senior management consultant, he understood that someone else would need to lead the charge forward. Stating that "he should get out of the way to make room for people with fresh ideas," Martino declined the invitation to join the newly formed Friends board. Nevertheless, he had started the ball rolling, and his quest for detailed information put subsequent efforts to revitalize Ellisville Marsh on a solid, historical footing.

Each of the founding directors had a different stake and interest in participating. For some it was the threat the eroding bluff posed to their homes. For others it was their family's strong connection to the salt marsh over generations. Each brought a distinctly personal perspective, a characteristic that would add depth and strength to the board's decision-making as the inlet maintenance project unfolded and challenges began to appear.

The only common thread among the founders was that all five owned homes on Lookout Point, the length of which was threatened by the unchecked migration of the salt marsh inlet. Three came from families that had been in Ellisville for more than a generation—Ellen Russell, Bob Goldthwaite, and Jack Scambos.

The Founders

Ellen Russell's roots in Ellisville extend back to 1903 when her great-grandparents bought property from Percy Marsh. Her three children are the fifth generation in the family to grow up here. By virtue of their summer experiences living next to the salt marsh and the fact that two of them have done fieldwork for the Friends, they are the most closely connected to Ellisville Marsh of anyone in their generation.

Bob Goldthwaite's parents built their house on Lookout Point seventy years ago, around 1950. Bob was one of the local teenagers who harvested sea moss from Ellisville Marsh during the summers of 1955 through 1957. Until recently, he continued to live in the same house overlooking the sea.

Jack Scambos's maternal grandparents built their cottage five years after the Goldthwaites, before Jack was born. He shares touching stories of his coming-of-age experiences in the marsh and neighborhood.

The Hruby family arrived in 1991 when Peter was still a teenager. That was the year Hurricane Bob crashed into the New England coast and diverted the Ellisville Marsh channel by more than a thousand feet. The cottage his parents had only recently purchased ended up being the most directly threatened of any on Lookout Point by that event.

My own arrival on the scene in 2003 made me the newcomer, the one least familiar with Ellisville's rich history, eager to learn from others' stories and experiences.

Following the tone set by its founders, the Friends have always operated as a consensus-based organization. Although disagreements sometimes arise about the best way to pursue the outcome everyone wants—a healthy salt marsh ecosystem of plants, wildlife, and fisheries preserved for future generations—the board comes together when necessary to overcome barriers and find the resources necessary to move ahead. The project is led by people who bring a diversity of perspectives but also a willingness to listen and engage in discussion and debate. Mutual respect built up over many years enables this balance to be maintained.

None of the five original board members had any idea they would still be working on the Ellisville Marsh project fifteen years later or that four of them would still be serving on the board. Would any have signed up knowing that such a seemingly manageable task would take more than a decade with an end still not in sight?

Russell was unquestionably the one with the most relevant knowledge and insights on the inaugural board. She had summered in Ellisville all her life, and her parents had built a home on the knoll at the eastern end of the marsh where bald eagles can sometimes be spotted in the trees. At the time of the Friends' founding, Ellen's children were of school age, and she had returned to graduate school at the University of Massachusetts–Amherst to earn a doctorate in plant and soil sciences. The studies she was conducting in the marsh every summer to satisfy her degree requirements would lend themselves to environmental monitoring requirements under the Friends' regulatory permits, ensuring the continuity of her scientific data gathering. And her family's expanding involvement created hope for the future. From the time in 2007 when her then-young children trooped into the marsh with her, armed with fishing nets, until they became environmental interns in successive summers ten years later, the Friends' leadership harbored the hope that one of them might ultimately join the board and carry on the work. Not-very-subtle suggestions to this effect have been made.

One might guess that Jack Scambos joined the Friends' board because his family's cottage enjoyed a picturesque view of the marsh inlet. To get the best view from his yard, one need only stand in the spot where an old, earthen gun emplacement once stood watch for German submarines during World War II. But Scambos had another motivation. He is intrigued by complex engineering challenges, especially those involving water. This is what brought him to the Friends and continues to drive him so many years later.

Scambos founded Aqueous Recovery Resources, Inc., in 1990 to target the emerging market in industrial water recycling and reuse. He holds nine patents and several global trademarks on technology used in the separation and recovery of oil and similar contamination from water. Of course, none of this was known when he joined the board. He is that kind of person.

Scambos sees water scarcity and compromised water resources as a growing, existential threat in many parts of the world. In addition to serving on the Friends' board, which he stepped up to lead for several years, he also serves on the board of advisors at the University of Vermont College of Engineering and Mathematical Sciences.

Scambos's diligence in contracting when it comes to reopening the Ellisville inlet and his innate understanding of the natural forces that operate at the inlet add significant value to the organization. He can be counted on to challenge the thinking of other members of the board during discussions of hard engineering issues (reinforced structures like groins, jetties, and revetments) or soft solutions (living coastline approaches, e.g., strategically placed seeding with native plants, oyster beds, and offshore devices that diminish wave energy).

At the time of the Friends' formation, Pete Hruby had assumed the role of president of LOPIA, succeeding Martino. However, it seems to have been preordained that he would carry on after the Hrubys' lengthy struggle with the MassDEP that led to the Friends' creation. He took on and continues to oversee the electronic presence of the organization, maintaining the website, setting up electronic member payment options, and advising on all manner of digital technologies. An information technology entrepreneur at the time the organization was founded, his work for the Friends was a natural complement to his professional interests at the time.

Hruby cajoled his sister, Adela, into designing the organization's graphic logo and developing the group's digital brochure. The Hrubys, along with the Martinos, the Russell/Foleys, and others, exemplify what keeps the Friends and the Ellisville Marsh revitalization project going—different members of a family pitch in when another skill set is required. Environmental action in Ellisville is a family thing, an intergenerational affair. One person's connection with nature propagates through the family tree.

Bob Goldthwaite, the fourth member of the Friends' original board, is a retired engineer who specialized in breweries. He, too, spent his childhood summers in Ellisville and shares his memories of harvesting sea moss as a teenager. He brought an engineer's persistence in asking detailed questions about what the Friends were planning to do and how it would work. Although he is no longer on the board, he remains a member.

My own motivation to be a founding board member was simple. I was compelled by what I had seen happening at the salt marsh inlet in late 2003 and inspired by the old-timers' stories. Maintaining the tidal inlet seemed a worthwhile cause. Moreover, I had significant experience in regulatory affairs from my days working at the New England Electric System that I imagined might prove useful in permitting.[3] Little did I know at the time that gaining the permits for something as modest as reopening a blocked salt marsh inlet could turn out to be as challenging as some of the regulatory back-and-forth I had engaged in when I worked for a $3 billion electric utility.

Subsequent additions to the board illustrate the breadth of talent and diversity of perspectives that have been drawn to the project. Current and former board members reflect a diverse set of talents: Paula Marcoux is a cooking authority, author, and editor; Diane Jordan, a landscaper, outdoorswoman, and sailor; Brad Winn, a noted expert on migratory shorebirds at Manomet, an environmental nonprofit; Kelley O'Neel, a clinical psychologist; Frank Doyle, a certified public accountant and financial analyst; Susan Pleadwell, a professional editor with long-standing family ties to the area; Peter Schwartzman, a licensed hydrogeologist; Henry Riter, who works in the investment and pension services industry and is an avid scuba diver; Becky Harris, former director of Mass Audubon's Coastal Waterbird Program; Kim Tower, an environmental technician with the Town of Plymouth.

Highly skilled people proved more than willing to commit their energy, skills, and enthusiasm to such a compelling environmental project. Once on board, they inevitably formed their own unique, personal connections. The Friends did not ask for resumes. Those who showed up simply filled roles that needed filling. Their areas of expertise and interest became apparent.

The Friends' experience has also shown that people who highly value the natural environment have nuanced views. They constantly pose questions. What is the right balance between protecting a natural place and allowing people to actively experience it? At what point does human intervention become excessive and disrupt the underlying natural balance? Are the most sustainable solutions to problems like blockage of a tidal inlet hardened (made of boulders and concrete) or soft (dune nourishment, revegetation, and artificial oyster beds)? Do crowded beaches deter shorebird nesting or help keep predators at bay?[4] Having a diverse set of opinions on the leadership team helps a project navigate carefully and wisely. It is not always easy though.

A Like-Minded Community

The Friends' community of supporters turned out to be much like its board. The project has attracted some two hundred members over the years. A close-knit group of about twenty-five people performs most of the actual work. The rest provide financial support through membership dues and, in some cases, more generous gifts. Others make their own unique contributions.

Mike Brennan and his wife live thirty miles away in Fairhaven, Massachusetts. Brennan owns a small plane and looks for excuses to fly. Ellisville Marsh is one of them. Several times a year the Friends receive an email from him with a link to online photos. The images of the marsh Brennan has captured, sometimes while leaning out of the cockpit to get a clear view under the wing strut, have been invaluable in seeing the totality of the salt marsh and barrier beach system. He flies lower than the aircraft that serves as the platform for the more technical, aerial orthophotos the Friends have commissioned and higher than the drones people use to capture bird's-eye view videos from above the salt marsh.

More than a decade ago, when Brennan flew low over the Plymouth coastline in midsummer, his view of Ellisville Marsh was breathtaking. His camera captured what most of us had already noticed—that the marsh looked healthier than it had in many years. Thick saltmarsh cordgrass was popping up in new places that twelve months earlier had been bare mudflats. Cordgrass also seemed to be repopulating areas in the back marsh where most of the vegetation had died off. The images lent credence to claims that the Friends' inaugural reopening of the blocked salt marsh inlet had improved environmental conditions.

Brennan's view from one or two thousand feet above the salt marsh highlights things that cannot be seen on the ground or from a boat on the water. Each successive series of photos has captured the imagination. Viewing his aerial images is like taking a ride on a magic carpet over a natural kingdom. Some of his photographs have even played a key role as evidence in resolving differences of opinion between the Friends and regulatory agencies.

A similarly fresh perspective has been brought to the project by young people who have been engaged by the Friends as summer interns since 2014. An original goal of creating a "living laboratory" or "open-air classroom" at Ellisville Marsh has not been realized for a variety of reasons, the most practical of which is that there are no restrooms for schoolchildren on the property. Nevertheless, environmental data collection work in the summer has turned out to be an opportunity for college students studying environmental science or a related major to gain valuable field experience.

The Friends' summer interns have deployed underwater pressure gauges to determine daily tidal ranges, taken water samples to determine salinity and water quality, and surveyed the prevalence of vegetation in monitoring plots across the marsh. It is tedious work in sometimes-stifling conditions. Sarah Cowles, the Friends' first environmental intern in 2014, is now a middle-school science teacher in Lewiston, Maine.

In subsequent summers, the Friends looked for college students closer to home to avoid the need to find temporary housing for an intern from outside the area. The aforementioned Abby Foley filled the role for the next four summers. Foley's final-year capstone project at the University of New Hampshire was titled "The Effects of Tidal Inlet Maintenance Dredging on the Productivity and Health of Ellisville Marsh Based on the Growth of Primary Vegetation Species and Other Environmental Parameters." Foley entered nursing school following graduation.

The Friends next tapped Foley's younger brother to collect the environmental monitoring data. The Friends asked Chris Foley to describe what he learned during his internship summer in 2019:

I will be honest, I did not know too much about what I was getting myself into when I accepted the offer. However, once getting out on the marsh I really started to enjoy the things I was exposed to. I learned so much I never would have without the experience. The names of all the different marsh plants are still floating around in my head. Along with the species of plants, I learned all about how to take salinity measurements, how to use HOBO® loggers and the software associated, and much more. Not only did I learn things about the marsh, but also I learned how to manage my time better, how important responsibilities given to you are—all things that will help me throughout this school year and beyond. I could not be more grateful to the Friends of Ellisville Marsh for giving me this opportunity. I hope this becomes a lasting connection, and I look forward to doing more work and becoming more involved in the future.[5]

The purpose behind hiring college students as summer environmental interns, with preference given to those hailing from local families, is not very deeply hidden: to develop a generation of younger people who care deeply about this natural place and have had the opportunity to find their own personal connection. The Friends' board of directors is an older bunch. New blood is needed. Seeds have been planted. Succession planning is important in an organization involved in environmental stewardship, especially when a project might go on forever.

Seven years after her internship, Sarah Cowles described the impact that can come from connecting deeply with a special place like Ellisville Marsh:

I remember my time on the Ellisville Marsh very fondly. It was great to be able to use my previous experience to do something new that summer. I learned a lot about what different tools can be used to collect data, such as the HOBO data loggers, and about how the tides themselves work. I have a lot of memories that are connected to the marsh. The one that sticks out to me is one particularly hot day that I needed to dig on the beach to find an elevation marker and how excited I was to finally find it! Since then, I've taken a job as a middle school science teacher in Lewiston, Maine. My experience with the marsh definitely gave me an edge when I was applying for teaching jobs, because it meant that I had real-world experience to bring into the classroom. I'm working on getting a couple of HOBO loggers for my classroom so that we can track real-time data for the meteorology unit that we do in eighth grade.[6]

The people who founded the Friends, the volunteers, the old-timers, and the summer environmental interns all saw Ellisville Marsh as a natural place that could be brought back, revitalized. Little did any of them know how personal an interest they would come to have. Or how invested in the project they would become. Or how challenging a task this might ultimately turn out to be.

CHAPTER 6

A Thousand Paper Cuts

THE FRIENDS' REGULATORY EXPERIENCE is a cautionary tale for anyone planning to pursue environmental permits in Massachusetts. A person who actually understands what will be required to safely navigate through the regulatory minefield and emerge at the other end with all the necessary permits might well decide not to proceed in the first place.

To earn the regulatory permits needed to reopen and maintain the blocked Ellisville Marsh inlet, five stops had to be made along the way, each one capable of derailing the project. That initial journey took the Friends more than two years, and the cost of acquiring all the permits ended up nearly double the total cost of performing the actual work over the first ten years of the project's life. What is wrong with this picture? In a word: everything.

Death from a thousand paper cuts. Running the gauntlet. Navigating a minefield. Any of these clichéd expressions might fairly describe the process by which environmental permits are issued in Massachusetts. The journey from start to finish can be a long haul. Applicants with low levels of patience are likely to find themselves left unsatisfied, if not unsuccessful, at the end of the process.

Traveling down this road is not for the faint of heart. Dogged determination does not begin to describe what is required to gain the permits needed to reopen a blocked tidal inlet in

Massachusetts. Perseverance alone is insufficient. At some point in the process, one may decide that permitting must be completed simply to prove it *can* be done. For a project site located within an area of critical environmental concern (ACEC), the stakes are even higher and the odds of success lower. That a small, community nonprofit rather than a municipality or commercial entity might undertake such a project was almost unheard of when the Friends launched its permitting quest.

Permitting agencies did not quite know how to view the Friends. Nor did the nonprofit's permitting team know what to expect. Would regulatory agencies question the organization's altruistic-sounding motives? Drag the process out until the money was gone? Or would a public official emerge who might be willing to champion the project?

Time and money must be invested in equally large amounts when one seeks environmental permits in Massachusetts. A phalanx of regulatory bodies and sister agencies weighs in during the proceedings, raising the stakes. When all permits were finally in hand allowing the blocked Ellisville Marsh inlet to be reopened after a two-year permitting struggle, David Gould observed, "That was fast." He would know, having permitted multiple coastal and riverine projects over the years. The cost was another matter.

No one in the Friends' organization expected at the outset that it would end up costing so much. The project team certainly should have known. Vlad Hruby had spent even more for his emergency one-time-only permits to reopen the inlet and save his house from falling onto the beach a few years earlier.

Avoiding a Knockout in Round One

To kick off the environmental permitting process in Massachusetts, one must file an Environmental Notification Form (ENF) with the Massachusetts Environmental Policy Act Office (MEPA), part of the Executive Office of Energy and Environmental Affairs.

Success or failure at MEPA can be summed up simply: Will an environmental impact report (EIR) be required before the project can move on to the actual permitting steps or not?

Preparing an EIR can be an expensive, time-consuming, and contentious affair, so this outcome is to be avoided. In the Friends' case, a Notice of Project Change (NPC) was submitted because Vlad Hruby had already filed an ENF to reopen the Ellisville Marsh inlet several years earlier. Because of this, the regulatory agencies treated it as an existing project. The Friends were picking it up from Hruby.

It was subsequently determined that the project existed on paper long before Hruby's 2002 permit application. Plans for work on the Ellisville inlet were found to exist as far back as 1917. The old plans were evidence that the Friends were continuing a long-standing inlet maintenance project. The fact that the old plans had been developed by a state agency—the Massachusetts Commission on Waterways and Public Lands—should have facilitated permitting of the project. It did not however.

The Friends' NPC stated that erosion of the coastal bank was no longer the driving factor behind the project, as by 2008 the focus had shifted to restoring the health of fisheries and wildlife in the salt marsh. Hruby's 2003 work had relieved the pressure on the coastal bank. The filing was accompanied by an existing conditions survey plan and project engineering plan, each of which cost several thousand dollars to prepare. The former showed in graphic detail what was there, whereas the latter described how it was to be altered.

Fortunately, expensive permit plans can be reused in subsequent permit proceedings with other local, state, and federal agencies. Taking over responsibility for the project meant the Friends would replace Hruby as the responsible project owner and permit holder. But this time the project would be for ongoing maintenance.

That Vlad Hruby had undertaken his project in advance of the Friends was a blessing. Notwithstanding the discovery of the old plans, he had established an official permitting record that could be continued. This spared the Friends having to start from scratch, not that the permitting burden would turn out to be any less. It simply made permitting feasible. Starting from the beginning with a proposed project located within an ACEC might very well have been an impossible feat to accomplish.

The project area would be confined to a one-acre footprint. Up to thirty-six hundred cubic yards of material was to be excavated from the blocking spit to re-create a straight-line channel path for the greatest tidal flow efficiency. The excavated sand would be moved to a location above the high-water level for beach nourishment. In this case, beach nourishment was not for erosion control but rather to enhance nesting habitat for shorebirds on endangered and threatened species lists, namely, Piping Plovers and Least Terns.

Beach nourishment with excavated sand was not the Friends' idea. The US Fish and Wildlife Service (USFWS) identified this as a must-have for the project to be approved. As the federal agency tasked with protecting threatened and endangered species, USFWS essentially held veto power over the project. The beach nourishment would enhance nesting habitat for threatened shorebirds. One pair of nesting birds, it turns out, can make or break the permitting process.

The Friends proposed to build a berm along the south side of the channel with excavated sand to hold the inlet in place. The berm would have a gently graded slope considered ideal for shorebird nesting, not more than one foot of rise for every ten feet of length. This specification came from USFWS guidelines and was incorporated into permits subsequently issued to the Friends for the project.

In fact, the agency's "Guidelines for Managing Recreational Activities in Piping Plover Breeding Habitat on the U.S. Atlantic Coast to Avoid Take under Section 9 of the Endangered Species Act" became an official part of the organization's permits, which seemed unnecessary. A Friends' team had already been protecting the birds and monitoring nests for several years by that time, trained by expert staff from Mass Audubon's Coastal Waterbird Program.[1]

Many public agencies weigh in during MEPA proceedings. Some make advisory recommendations to the regulatory authority that ultimately issues the permits. Others use the proceedings to make their wish list of requirements stick because MEPA's leverage over project proponents is so significant.

A favorable MEPA decision is do-or-die for a small project. If the Friends' project had been subjected to an EIR requirement, the cost of compliance could have exceeded the cost of performing the project over many years. Fortunately though, that was not to be the case.

During the MEPA process, a situation arose in which two state agencies publicly stated their opposition to the project to restore Ellisville Marsh. The offices of president of the Senate Therese Murray, Representative Vinny deMacedo, and Lieutenant Governor Timothy Murray took an active position on behalf of the Friends during this process, and the favorable outcome was undoubtedly due in no small part to their interventions.

Many Friends members took the time to write letters to the MEPA office and/or the Plymouth Conservation Commission. Supporting letters were also sent in by the Village of Cedarville Steering Committee; David Gould; and Ed Reiner.

In September 2008 the Massachusetts secretary of energy and environmental affairs issued the project a MEPA (Massachusetts Environmental Policy Act) certificate stating that an environmental impact report (EIR) would not be required for the project to proceed to permitting.

While the MEPA decision waived the requirement for an EIR, several important conditions were laid out in the decision letter. Most important to subsequent permitting activities was the stipulation that an interagency process should be undertaken "for pre-application review and permitting review" before the Massachusetts Department of Environmental Protection (MassDEP) could issue its two state permits.

Five state agencies, with a potpourri of acronyms—DCR, MassDEP, MDMF, NHESP and MCZM—were to work with the Friends of Ellisville Marsh to "develop data monitoring requirements for the Ellisville Marsh and barrier beach system."[2] The MEPA letter, which was signed by the Massachusetts secretary of energy and environmental affairs, went on to say that financing of the "endeavor" should come from the interagency group. It was unclear what that meant.

Friends board members never got their hopes up that financial assistance would be forthcoming from the public sector. This turned out to be a prudent position because the group has not received any federal, state, or local government funding since its inception.[3] Every dollar of the Friends' funding has come instead from hard-earned private donations and grants. More than $200,000. Ten corporate and institutionally funded grants and more than seven hundred individual donations have been received over the years. The latter category accounts for the bulk of the organization's total funding.

It was during this interagency review that project plans surfaced showing that the Commonwealth of Massachusetts and the Town of Plymouth had periodically dredged the inlet since 1917. One of the Friends' arguments had been that it was simply asking to return to the more responsible environmental stewardship practices of the past, so these plans were a key discovery and essentially counted as evidence of regulatory permits. As such, the Friends were able to submit permit applications that built on a historical pattern of inlet maintenance, significantly reducing the burden of proof.

The First Interagency Review Process

The interagency review process ordered by MEPA was, in spite of the Friends' best hopes, a torturous and inefficient affair that lasted for six months beginning in late 2008 and ending in the spring of the following year. If the group's representatives had not bundled together a consensus list of monitoring requirements into a neat package and declared the process to be successfully wrapped up that spring, it might never have ended.

Staffers from the various agencies came to meetings largely unprepared to discuss the specific issues that had been sent to them ahead of time with the meeting agenda. Some evidently had not read any of the advance materials before the meetings. No one from the public agencies appeared to have an inclination to manage the process toward tangible results or meet any sort of time line.

The Friends' oft-repeated pitch to the assembled group, which was generally made up of fifteen or so agency people, including interns and new hires brought along for training purposes, was, "You need to tell us what we will need to do to satisfy the permit requirements." The response to this simple and direct question on some days seemed to be, "Everything." On other days, it sounded more like, "You tell us." One got the impression that the agency people had never been in an interagency process before, which seemed highly unlikely.

Some of the representatives' recommended actions would have been nixed by other representatives in the room had they listened to what was being said, leaving it to Friends members to point out the conflicts. For example, one agency representative would insist on placement of excavated sand in a certain location; another would explain why sand could not be placed in that location. Both parties were in the room, seemingly unable to hear what their counterparts from sister agencies were saying.

The essence of the problem with environmental regulation in Massachusetts is that some of the agencies that participate in the process operate like sovereign nations, each protecting its own territory—water quality, marine mammals, fish, shellfish, threatened birds, plant life, eelgrass. Although some, like the Massachusetts Office of Coastal Zone Management, appeared to be structured in a way that is intended to overcome this, it did not work that way in practice. These agencies must defend regulations that have not kept up with changing realities—sea level rise, "nature-based" coastal solutions, and an explosion of new technologies.

Individuals within these agencies have wide latitude to push project requirements in directions that reflect their own preferences, which can be narrow and insulated. The salt marsh system and barrier beach in Ellisville is a complex combination of natural resources. None of these can be parsed and considered separately, yet that is how the process unfolded. Nature is tightly interconnected, but the regulatory process intended to protect it is highly compartmentalized.

Environmental regulations appear to be applied differently at restoration projects in tidally restricted salt marshes across the state. Rumney Marsh, north of Boston, was designated a Massachusetts ACEC in 1988. The salt marsh is, according to USEPA–New England, one of the most biologically significant salt marshes north of Boston. In some ways it is similar to Ellisville Marsh, only much larger, covering 2,274 acres.

Rumney Marsh is the site of a waste-to-energy facility, a trash-burning incinerator that produces a large volume of toxic fly ash. The material is stored in a landfill on-site. The state ordered the operation to be shut down in 1996. However, the site license was subsequently extended in 1997, and the MassDEP has since allowed the operator to amend its permit and expand the site multiple times. After reports of illegal dumping of toxic water and sludge into the marsh surfaced in 2011, the operator paid a $7.5 million fine to the MassDEP, the largest in state history at the time.[4]

At Rumney Marsh the fly ash disposal pit is not fully lined to protect against leaching of toxic heavy metals into the surrounding soil and salt marsh ecosystem. As a result, the plant's main by-product is likely to be poisoning the salt marsh around it. Looking at these two projects, it would appear that protection of the environment in Massachusetts is discretionary. A polluter is given wide latitude. An environmental nonprofit with no material self-interest is not.

One telling experience during the Friends' arduous journey through the permitting maze involved the lengths to which the organization might have been required to go to monitor the health of offshore eelgrass. Those in state government whose job it is to focus on eelgrass did not express any particular interest in salt marsh plants or wildlife during the interagency meetings. In any event, the Friends had no quarrel with watching over the eelgrass bed. Eelgrass is an important resource for fish and shellfish—juvenile lobsters find safe haven in it. The issue was: What can reasonably be expected of a small nonprofit with no paid staff that receives no public funding?

Representatives from Mass Fisheries, the state agency charged with monitoring eelgrass, laid out a plan that would have required the Friends to contract with a team of professional divers to swim underwater transects through the eelgrass bed while operating video cameras and wearing GPS trackers. The imagery would be referenced to GPS data points so that a survey-quality, visual representation of the health of the bed could be developed.

What was proposed sounded expensive to the Friends. It appeared that no other salt marsh project in Massachusetts had previously been required to engage such a specialized dive team. Indeed, when the Friends researched the nationwide availability of dive teams that had done this sort of work, they found only one.

The Friends counterproposed that it would be within its means and capabilities to map the extent of the eelgrass bed with a handheld GPS device from a kayak on a day each summer when the tides would be at a cyclical low. In practical terms, Friends volunteers would be sitting in calm water right above the bed within a few feet of the shiny, light-green eelgrass shafts, producing a delineated map more accurate than the aerial surveillance the commonwealth had been doing of eelgrass beds along the coastline for years.

Ultimately, the MassDEP, the state's permitting body, denied its sister agency's request for the specialized dive team, and the Friends' approach was adopted as one of the permit conditions. But the sense of bullets whizzing by would continue throughout the remainder of the permitting process. How did the Friends bring closure to the interagency review? Its representatives took charge of the meetings, managed open items with tracking lists, and informed the assembled group when they believed consensus had been reached on individual items. No one disagreed with any of this.

For its part, Friends leadership was overly accommodating. In the end, the project team agreed to undertake nine separate environmental monitoring programs. Ellisville Marsh was on its way to becoming one of the most closely scrutinized salt marshes in the Commonwealth of Massachusetts.

Ironically, the highest resolution and most expensive monitoring technique the Friends employed over the years—aerial infrared, orthophotogrammetry—did not come up during the discussions.[5] The Friends' board unilaterally decided that periodic investments in ultrahigh-resolution imagery would produce the greatest return in terms of documenting conditions in the marsh. For the work, the Friends contracted with Col-East, an aerial photogrammetry firm operating out of North Adams, Massachusetts.

The Friends commissioned aerial orthos in 2008, 2011, and 2018 and submitted the resulting imagery to the agencies. The digital image captured in late 2018 alone was 1,300 megabytes in size and cost over $2,000, including the cost of the aircraft and pilot for the overflight. For its 2008 work, Col-East donated the cost of the flight and photography, significantly reducing the overall expense. The images were all taken within an hour of low tide to provide the greatest visibility. When the tide is out, one can see almost everything. Analysis of the aerial imagery enabled comparison of the extent and health of marsh vegetation over time, particularly after the channel inlet had been reopened.

Gaining the Local Wetlands Permit

On the project went. The next stop was the Plymouth Conservation Commission, the project's local permitting authority. The role of conservation commissions throughout Massachusetts is to protect natural resources, particularly wetlands, through enforcement of the Massachusetts Wetlands Protection Act. Working with the commission was a relief in an otherwise arduous permitting journey. This did not happen by chance.

The organization was shepherded through the commission's permitting process by Randy Parker, owner of a local survey firm, Land Management Systems, Inc. Parker is a well-known local personality. His sometimes unruly shock of white hair and lanky frame make him easy to spot in a crowd. He has performed work all over town and is respected by town officials for his expansive knowledge.

It helps that Parker has a gift for explaining technical issues. His soft-spoken New England drawl seems to help in this regard, calming the room where the commission meets to review permit applications. More important, he knows Ellisville Marsh as well as the old lobstermen did. He understands how the inlet works and why keeping it open is vital. Every once in a while, he can be seen sailing his beloved catboat off Ellisville. Parker is a guardian angel of this place.

A detailed Notice of Intent application had to be filed with the commission, but it mainly repeated what was said in the MEPA and the MassDEP submissions. Each of these applications has unique requirements and format, akin to college applications before the introduction of the Common Application in 1975. Although the Friends' project was favorably reviewed and approved by the Conservation Commission in a mercifully short period of time, there was a drawback: the new permit would expire in three years. But the inlet maintenance project might last forever.

Next Stop: State Permits

Next up among the permitting agencies once MEPA had been safely passed and the Conservation Commission had granted its Order of Conditions was the MassDEP, which required two separate permits before federal permitting could commence. One is called a Chapter 91 Waterways Permit, the other a Section 401 Water Quality Certification (WQC). Different sections of the MassDEP, one in Boston and the other in Lakeville, would judge the project's fitness for their respective permits. All the Friends' board knew at the start of this phase was that it had been the lack of a final WQC that had caused Vlad Hruby so much grief in 2005.

The two permit applications were submitted in May 2009. The Friends engaged a local consulting firm, LEC Environmental Consultants, to assist in preparation of the initial applications. In such things experience really matters. More than one person in permitting agencies had been heard to say early on that they "prefer dealing with professionals."

The process the Friends observed seemed to be optimized for career agency staffers and expensive, outside consultants. Both sides have a vested self-interest in keeping it that way. This is not to say the Friends were dissatisfied with the work LEC did on its behalf. The firm's principal, Stan Humphries, was well versed in the proposed work, understood the permitting process, and was responsive to the Friends' needs and budget limitations.

The process of environmental permitting in Massachusetts is a back-and-forth tug-of-war between a project proponent and those who either do not want the project to go forward or want specific and sometimes onerous conditions imposed. In the case of the Ellisville Marsh inlet maintenance project, no abutting property owners or other individuals were opposed. In fact, no one intervened to oppose what the Friends proposed to do. A high percentage of the people who lived within a mile or so of Ellisville Marsh were Friends' donors, project supporters, or volunteers.

Opposition to the project and concern over its potential impacts was limited to a small number of Massachusetts state agencies or, more precisely, a few individuals within the agencies. A couple of agency staffers publicly expressed their desire to adopt the "Do nothing and let nature take its course" approach. This might have been an appropriate position if their predecessors in state government had not constructed a rock jetty on the northern side of the inlet that massively disrupts the natural sediment flow along the coast and contributes to the inlet blockages. They argued that Ellisville Marsh is, in fact, or used to be, or wants to be, a salt pond. This, too, was hard to accept, given that maps of the area back to the early 1700s prominently feature an inlet.

During an early site meeting with a handful of key agency people, one staffer from the state's ACEC program claimed that a permit had "never been issued for such a project within an ACEC." In fact, a project on a barrier beach within the Pleasant Bay ACEC in Chatham had been making its way through the approval process for nearly a year before the meeting took place. The project had already received a favorable MEPA decision and was issued its Chapter 91 permit by the MassDEP a few months later, a year and a half ahead of the Ellisville Marsh inlet project.

More frustrating for the Friends was the realization that the project was being impeded by people working under a state program with a seemingly supportive mission statement. "The purpose of the Areas of Critical Environmental Concern (ACEC) Program is to preserve, restore, and enhance critical environmental resources and resource areas of the Commonwealth of Massachusetts," reads the program's website. A project to revitalize fisheries and wildlife in a damaged salt marsh seemed to be closely aligned with the program's core interests.

The Friends' team never came to understand why individuals within some Massachusetts state agencies did not embrace the project. The interagency process that began shortly after MEPA signaled there would be ongoing resistance to the project. Was it because they did not create the project, fund it, or control it?

Some of the agency people threw brickbats at the project, perhaps hoping the Friends would give up and go away. But they under-estimated the depth of the group's commitment to addressing the long-standing problem at the salt marsh inlet.

The Friends completed the final applications to the MassDEP for a Chapter 91 Waterways Permit and WQC after an eight-month-long pursuit. In the filing, the organization provided detailed descriptions of nine environmental monitoring programs that would be ongoing throughout the term of the channel main-tenance permits, then assumed to be five years. This represented an extraordinary commitment for a permit applicant, especially a small nonprofit whose only reward would be the satisfaction of knowing that it had intervened to help the salt marsh regain much of its former vitality.

The project ultimately received both of its required MassDEP permits, but only after the ante was upped as far as collection of environmental monitoring data was concerned. Looking back, one marvels at the requirements state agencies imposed on the project. One had to do with determining the sizes of grains of sand. The MassDEP required the Friends to bring in a backhoe for a day to dig down eight feet and bag samples of material, almost exclusively sand, at the location where they proposed to breach the barrier spit and restore the inlet. The purpose of this sampling and laboratory analysis was to show that the sediment to be excavated was compatible with sand where it was to be placed for beach nourishment and shorebird nesting habitat, about a hundred yards away.

Pointing out that thirty-six hundred cubic yards of sand is a modest amount by nature's standards—a single storm can move five times that volume of sand around Ellisville beach—the Friends requested a waiver of the requirement, which was summarily rejected. The sand's compatibility had to be quan-titatively determined. The excavator and labor together cost $1,500 for the day's work. The lab provided a size distribution report: 99.8 percent of the material that had been dug up and placed in bags was in fact sand, with grains sized between 0.5 and 2.0 millimeters, aka "gravely sand." One wonders: Should this have come as a surprise, on a beach? Was it worth $1,500 to discover this fact?

The now-retired agency staff person who denied the Friends' request for waiver of the sampling requirement appears to have visited the Ellisville Marsh inlet for the first time a few years after his waiver denial. That visit was made to investigate a complaint that a throng of mice had invaded a home a half mile from the site of inlet excavation work on one of the coldest days of that winter. The claim was that somehow the clamor of the excavators had disturbed the mice's winter reverie and chased them indoors. The investigation found no fault on the Friends' part. Perhaps the mice were just cold.

Last Stop: Federal Permit

The final leg of the permitting journey was the US Army Corps of Engineers (USACE), the federal agency responsible for projects conducted in US waters, including tidal areas such as the Ellisville Marsh inlet. The project needed a Massachusetts general permit from the USACE. Fortunately, the project was small enough that the existing packet of plans and information would suffice for project review, even if the entire application would span a hundred pages.

Who needed to receive copies of the USACE permit application? Tribal historic preservation officers in Massachusetts and Rhode Island, the Massachusetts Board of Underwater Archaeological Resources, and a host of other agencies, some of which only confirmed receipt of their copy long after the permit itself was issued. One Rhode Island tribe sent a letter a year after the permit was issued saying it had no problem with the project.

As it turned out, review of the project by the USACE was completed expeditiously, as the agency's project manager was already familiar with the site. In fact, the Friends relied on his aerial photographs of the marsh for a number of years. Unfortunately, this individual moved on to another assignment within the agency shortly thereafter, and his deep understanding of the project and site conditions went with him. Loss of agency officials familiar with the site and the project would become a familiar pattern over the next ten years.

The Friends learned during initial permitting and had the lesson reinforced throughout several rounds of repermitting that a single individual in a regulatory agency can help speed approval of a project like this. Conversely, another might hold it up for a year or more simply by imposing capricious and burdensome requirements that can cost a small nonprofit dearly. If certain officials had taken the time to visit the site, they likely would have realized why some of their agency's typical requirements made no sense. Perhaps the Friends would not have had to dig up sand on the barrier spit to prove it was compatible with sand on the beach a hundred yards away.

Only the End of the Beginning

For the Friends, earning the four original permits marked neither the end of the journey nor the beginning of the end. As Churchill famously suggested, it may have been only the end of the beginning. Each of the original permits came with a term of between three and five years, unfortunate in that the Friends would need to shoulder the burden of renewing each permit every few years.

To make matters worse, the permits were not synchronized. They expired at different times, creating a more or less continuous workload of tackling the next-in-line permit renewal. These permit renewals, reauthorizations, and extensions were needed because none of the permit-granting authorities recognized the fundamental nature of the project—*ongoing* maintenance of a marsh inlet, as the project was consistently presented by the Friends. None of the permitting agencies were able to adapt their permitting process to reflect this. When inquiries were made about the feasibility of ten-year permits, the common response was that it had not been done before and was therefore not allowed.

The Chapter 91 waterways permit issued in 2010 by the MassDEP contained an unusual condition: after the first three years of inlet maintenance, the agency would review the vast trove of environmental monitoring data that had been collected (also unusual for small marsh restoration projects) and decide whether to let the Friends continue exercising its permit authority. This condition was triggered in March 2013.

Another Interagency Review

The midterm review that had been written into the MassDEP permits may have reflected a lack of confidence on the state's part that a small nonprofit would adhere to all the rules and remain in full compliance with permit conditions. This review became another torturous affair, three years into the five-year permit term.

Some of the participating agency staffers tried to use the occasion of the review to redefine what success meant, what additional requirements should be imposed, and who should be responsible for analyzing the vast trove of environmental data being collected. Was the project's underlying objective to protect the marsh ecosystem from further damage due to periodic inlet blockage or to enhance fisheries and wildlife? Proving scientifically that the project had enhanced natural resources was difficult, if not impossible, after a period as short as three years.

Attempts to redefine the project's objectives midstream happened partly because new people had joined the agencies that advise the MassDEP. They were unfamiliar with the project's purpose, history, or site conditions. Some were fresh out of degree programs and new to regulatory work. Many appeared not to have visited the site.

It is worth pointing out that the Friends received good cooperation from the MassDEP itself and that the department treated the Ellisville Inlet Maintenance Project fairly and consistently. The same cannot be said of a number of other state agencies that participated in the permitting process and sought to layer on requirements in their strongly worded recommendations to the MassDEP.

The Friends summed up the second interagency review process at the time as follows:

> While we are pleased that the department has restored our authority to maintain the inlet for two more years and laid out a path that should allow maintenance work later in the winter, we were disappointed by a number of details in the decision and plan to follow up with the department accordingly. Details of our concerns . . . can be summarized as follows:
>
> - The decision puts even greater burdens on the shoulders of our small, nonprofit organization in the areas of data collection, reporting, and scientific analysis.
>
> - If the decision stands as currently written, it will shorten the term of our Chapter 91 waterways permit by four years, from 2019 to 2015.
>
> - The process outlined for requesting permission to perform work in February or March introduces uncertainty to our planning for maintenance events.[6]

Over the next decade, the Friends would outlast an entire generation of regulatory people, watching them come and go, while others retired. Agencies with significant technical capabilities of their own attempted to make the Friends responsible for what they referred to as "data synthesis," the detailed analysis of data that had been collected to determine trends and, ideally, uncover cause-and-effect relationships.

The key question was always: "Does maintaining the Ellisville Marsh inlet help or hurt the health of fisheries and wildlife in the salt marsh?" Statements had already been publicly made by scientists and environmental engineers that the answer is an unequivocal "yes." However, proving this scientifically is difficult without a minimum of ten years of environmental data and sophisticated analytic capabilities.

A small nonprofit with no paid staff could not hope to marshal the resources to perform such analyses. Perhaps the suggestion had been made in hopes that the Friends could be found not to have upheld its end of the bargain. If so, the strategy failed.

The project ultimately scraped through, again. Thanks to Therese Murray, then the president of the Massachusetts senate, in whose district the project happened to lie, a meeting was set up with the secretary of energy and environmental affairs and key agency heads. The June 2014 meeting, which was held at the Massachusetts State House in Boston, led to the elimination of some of the more arcane and onerous monitoring requirements going forward. This was a theme noted several times during the project's life—with the involvement of senior policymaking officials, common sense became a factor, and roadblocks were removed. However, the potential value of the Ellisville Marsh Revitalization Project as a public-private partnership was never realized.

Meetings with elected state officials did not happen by chance or because any elected officials closely followed the progress of the marsh project. They only came about because of the persistent efforts of Friends member Greg Lano, from whose home on Lookout Point one views the shorebird nesting area in the foreground and the salt marsh inlet in the background.

For more than a decade, Lano has been relentless in his pursuit of the governor, lieutenant governor, Massachusetts senate president, and Plymouth's representatives in the statehouse. He built relationships with staff in each of their offices and managed to gain audiences when the project faced critical challenges from within the state bureaucracy. It is hard to imagine where the project would be today without his efforts. Lano became the project's "squeaky wheel." Environmental projects in Massachusetts do not necessarily succeed based on their merits alone.

Which monitoring programs were shelved after the 2014 statehouse meeting? Finfish counts, for one. It was impossible to net fish for sampling counts because there are so many side branches off the main marsh channel. Moreover, fishermen and -women balked at reporting how many fish they caught and where when they were asked to help. As one can imagine, such data are carefully guarded, considered trade secrets.

Shellfish sampling was also scrapped after two rounds of data collection. Clams were virtually nonexistent where the Friends had been ordered to sample, a reality confirmed by the consultant retained by the Friends. Beach transect measurements, which showed precisely where sand built up or was washed away, were discontinued as well after nearly ten years of semiannual data gathering.

Mostly, the Friends were unburdened of programs whose data had gone unused by state agencies for years. Data are shared on an annual basis with fifteen or more people spread across numerous local, state, and federal agencies. Yet gigabytes of data the Friends had been required to collect and submit were not reviewed by many of these agencies. This became evident because the file-sharing platform enabled the Friends to see when people who had been granted access to the online data repository actually went in to have a look.

A Never-Ending Process

A point of confusion inevitably arose when the Friends' project applied for renewal permits or permit extensions. As part of the application, the permitting agency expects to see an existing conditions plan that shows the compelling need for intervention. However, the Ellisville Marsh inlet undergoes routine maintenance on an as-needed basis, so if a survey team were to be sent to the site to prepare such an existing conditions plan it would, most of the time, suggest that nothing needed to be done.

Agency staffers who had not visited the site seemed perplexed by this. "Why do you need a permit?" was the implied reaction to permit renewal and extension requests. One adamantly insisted on a new survey plan in spite of being given a detailed explanation of why that would not create value for anyone. Photographs taken before and after maintenance should have been sufficient to demonstrate why the permit was needed. A brief site visit would have cleared up the confusion. But some key agency staff persons simply never found the time to make the trip.

Notwithstanding these challenges, the Friends' various permits had been renewed, reauthorized, or extended as many as four times by 2020. Several received automatic extension under provident state legislation, the Permit Extension Acts of 2010 and 2012. Even the COVID state of emergency that was declared in 2020 brought a state permit extension, buying the Friends some breathing room.

Most of the permitting work was performed by diligent members of the Friends' board. This required a substantial time commitment, thousands of hours in fact. By the point when the project's initial permits expired, some members of the Friends board had learned enough about the rules of the permitting process to know how to navigate it without outside assistance. Renewals and extensions of the four permits were at times straightforward, at others difficult and prolonged. The permit renewal process is onerous for a small, thinly funded nonprofit.

As the Friends' president, I became so worn out and disaffected by the constant permitting and repermitting work that I stepped down from the leadership role for several years. Fortunately, Jack Scambos picked up leadership responsibility for those years, a move that probably saved the organization.

The USACE permit, for example, was obtained without a lot of fuss in 2010 but followed an agonizing renewal process in 2015 that lasted about a year and caused the Friends to miss an inlet maintenance cycle. The Friends' initial five-year permit from the Army Corps of Engineers had expired in January 2015. In May the group submitted its application for a new permit, relying solely on internal expertise, saving several thousand dollars in the process. The application process dragged on into late 2015, and the application was posted for review by other federal agencies in November. The Friends finally received the new permit in March 2016, just three days before the maintenance contractor was to have moved his equipment onto the site. Sadly, this episode added to the experience that regulatory permitting had not become easier despite the project having by then been under way for more than five years.

Things did begin to get a little easier though. Extensions of the project's local Conservation Commission permit in 2017 and 2020 were straightforward affairs, a relief. The MassDEP permits were also extended for five years in 2019. The constructive manner in which this extension was handled by department officials reflected a newfound spirit of cooperation.

The second reauthorization of the Army Corps of Engineers' Massachusetts General Permit was also uncharacteristically straightforward. A letter request for reverification of the project's permit was submitted on behalf of the Friends by LEC Environmental and was quickly approved.

Had the project finally turned a corner? Was the project's sudden good fortune the result of different people handling the project within the respective regulatory agencies? Had the regulatory environment swung in a new direction? As the Friends learned, the permitting system's behavior is, if nothing else, unpredictable.

Why?

The reality is that each of the agencies the Friends has to deal with tends to think of permits, permit extensions, and renewals as one-time deals, notwithstanding that the Friends' project was clearly presented as an ongoing project with no end in sight. The environmental problem being addressed does not go away. There are other flaws in the permitting process as well.

Agency staffers were unable or unwilling to adapt their permitting processes for a project that is neither commercial, navigational, or recreational. The Ellisville Marsh inlet maintenance project was not undertaken to dredge a navigational channel or harbor or to construct a seawall to protect a coastal development.

There is no vested self-interest on the Friends' part, or on the part of individuals on its leadership team, beyond a collective desire for a healthy salt marsh full of fish and wildlife. The project is aimed solely at environmental revitalization of a natural resource the Friends do not own, for the benefit of the public-at-large. Yet the permitting process seemed more attuned to fending off commercial developments seen as hostile to the environment. Perhaps the Friends' project being small and ongoing explains the bureaucratic resistance and delays experienced throughout its fifteen-year life.

The Friends repeatedly sought to hold the Commonwealth of Massachusetts accountable for its past promises regarding development of a sustainable, long-term solution to the inlet blockage problem. Between the commonwealth's imperfect permitting process and its failure to live up to past promises, maintaining progress on a natural revitalization project acknowledged by virtually everyone to be in the public interest has been "like pulling teeth." Witnessing small steps toward the salt marsh regaining its former vibrancy makes it worth doing though.

By July of 2020 the Friends had begun pursuing an extension of their current regulatory permit from the Plymouth Conservation Commission, as it was scheduled to expire in September of that year. The commission acted in July to extend this permit for five additional years. All of the permits needed to continue maintaining the Ellisville Marsh inlet had now been extended, and Friends members could focus their attention and energy on programs.

Looking back over fifteen years, it is hard to comprehend that a project whose sole purpose was to maintain the tidal inlet of a Massachusetts coastal marsh, and whose proponents had no material or commercial self-interest, would encounter such unabated bureaucratic resistance. Yet it did. But once the regulatory permits were finally in hand, the real fun could begin.

CHAPTER 7

Breaching the Spit

⌐

Is YOUR ORGANIZATION PLANNING to bring an excavator and front-end loader onto a Massachusetts barrier beach to reopen a blocked salt marsh inlet? You finally have all the required regulatory permits in hand. You have raised the money to pay for the work. You have approved project plans. If only it were so easy.

The permits you worked so hard to obtain say only that the work is authorized. You have satisfied the *what*, the *where*, and the *why*. But not the *when*, the *how*, or the *by whom*. The key word, however, is still *if*.

Once the Friends had all regulatory permits required to reopen the Ellisville inlet in 2010, the organization shifted gears. Jack Scambos began requesting bids from construction firms to reopen the inlet. A bidders' meeting was held to obtain best and final bids. A pre-dredge shellfish survey inside Ellisville Harbor was completed by LEC Environmental. A punch list of compliance and reporting requirements stated in the permits was compiled to ensure that every step taken would be "by the book." And the group continued to seek additional funds to complete the initial stage of the marsh revitalization—reopening the blocked inlet. The Friends submitted more grant applications.

A myriad of permit conditions needed to be complied with to avoid running afoul of any one of a plethora of regulations. So many, in fact, that reopening the blocked inlet was, by the time it actually occurred in early 2011, anticlimactic. When could the work be done? Only in the dead of winter. What agency notifications needed to be made in advance? Several, all with different lead times. What kind of hydraulic fluid could be used in the equipment? Biodegradable only—vegetable oil, essentially. What environmental mitigation actions had to be taken? Deploy silt barriers or work only at dead low tides. Keep an oil spill kit on site at all times, and file an incident reporting procedure in case of a spill.

How was the work scheduled? It had to be completed within a five-consecutive-day window. How was the approved plan set on the physical site to guide the contractor? Volunteers redeployed the 2011 survey stakes using handheld GPS devices. What if the ground became so solidly frozen that the stakes could not be pounded in? Friends volunteers prayed for a warm day or planned to use painted rocks to mark property lines and channel reference points instead. What needed to happen after the work was completed? Post-dredge notifications had to be submitted to multiple agencies.

Many details had to be kept in mind. Every time since the initial maintenance work, preparatory tasks have been laid out in a detailed, multipage checklist. One misstep and the hard-earned permits are put at risk. Only after all the prerequisites have been checked off can work commence. The Friends repeated this drill seven times between 2011 and 2022.

Planning begins around Christmas, whether or not the salt marsh inlet is blocked, to be ready for whatever might unfold during the upcoming winter. One must guess at the probability that storms will block the inlet because no long-range weather forecast can accurately predict the odds. One proceeds with the expectation that maintenance will be required by late winter. The likelihood that a barrier spit will form and block the salt marsh inlet is fifty-fifty. Sometimes the barrier spit even starts to migrate back north toward the rock jetty, lessening the degree of tidal flow restriction, a form of self-healing.

Several of the permits prohibit inlet maintenance dredging

after January 31, so a request to waive this time-of-year restriction (TOY, to the regulators) is submitted early in the process. When granted, the TOY waiver allows work to occur until the end of March.[1] This substantially improves the Friends' odds of success for the inlet remaining open.

What is wrong with reopening the inlet in January? It is not the bitter cold—we are talking about hardy New Englanders here. Some, like board member Diane Jordan, simply shrug when asked to watch over maintenance work for several hours in near-zero temperatures with a bitter wind off the ocean. No, it is the likelihood that late-winter storms will reclose the inlet, wiping out January's inlet maintenance investment.

The scene on January 19, 2011, was memorable. For only the second time in almost twenty-five years, the blocked Ellisville inlet was reopened in its historical location, and tides once again flowed unrestricted into and out of the marsh. Cleansing of moribund areas of the marsh quickly became apparent—dead marsh grass clumps were seen floating out, the scouring of decayed material from the bottom was made apparent by a distinctive odor in the air. The Ellisville inlet had been diverted from its straight course out to Cape Cod Bay since early 2005, and marsh vegetation had continued its long-term decline, eventually exposing as much as ten acres of bare mudflats.

A contractor who understands coastal processes and knows how to take advantage of the tides had to be found and retained. The Friends were fortunate to have found one locally—a taciturn Yankee named Brian Richmond, the owner of George R. Richmond, Inc., of Manomet, one of Plymouth's villages. Brian and his sons tackle seawalls, jetties, and coastal reinforcement all over eastern Massachusetts. Although they use heavy equipment, they do so in a way that demonstrates their respect for the natural forces at play at each site, especially in a place as dynamic and challenging as the Ellisville Marsh inlet. And in the case of this project, they have shown they can be in and out in a matter of a few days.

The Richmonds work on the Ellisville Marsh inlet during morning low tides with outgoing tidal flows. This facilitates equipment access to the spit and minimizes the need to "dewater," or drain, the sand being removed. Sand that is loosened by the excavators is carried out to sea by the tide, not into the marsh where it could form shoals and provide a secondary restriction to the flow.

Practicality factors in here as well. At high tide, the channel that would need to be crossed by the equipment is six to eight feet deep and impassable. At low tide however, the stream is less than a foot deep, inches in some places. The maintenance work itself lasts two or three days. In the construction industry this job is considered pretty small. The Friends' 2011–12 inlet work was typical of what would occur many times over the next decade.

Thanks to the efficient, high-quality work of Brian Richmond and his sons and the capable supervision of Friends directors Jack Scambos, Paula Marcoux, Diane Jordan, and Frank Doyle, the Friends successfully completed that cycle of inlet maintenance on schedule and within budget in mid-January. Completing the work that year was essential, as tidal flows in the preceding few months had breached the channel wall, making blockage of the inlet much more likely to occur if the situation were left unaddressed. Scambos was again the overall strategist/tidal engineer, applying his understanding of the natural forces at work at the inlet and how to use them, rather than fight them.

The only hitches were a frozen fuel line on the diesel excavator the first morning (when the air temperature was a brisk seven degrees) and a flat tire on the loader two days later, both of which were fixed within an hour or two. Richmond lets half the air out of his loader's tires to work more effectively in the sand so the flat tire was not unusual. Members of the Friends' board stood supervisory watches in the bitter cold, warmed only by the satisfaction of seeing the water flowing rapidly out of the marsh again when the work was completed. The Richmonds' work done, the excavator made its way out the gate with a cacophony of squeaks and groans, leaving Ellisville Marsh peaceful and quiet once again.

A Harrowing Winter

The following winter of 2012–13, however, revealed to the Friends the full extent of challenges that would be associated with maintaining a New England salt marsh inlet. It was a harrowing time. Friends members began to understand that this would be a David and Goliath battle, with the marsh inlet and its stewards pitted against an often-furious sea.

Was that winter a harbinger of climate change or just a dramatic demonstration of Nature's erratic behavior? We will never know. One thing is for certain though: throughout that winter the coast of Massachusetts was battered and bruised by a series of severe, if not historic, storms, beginning in late October.

The storms arrived one after the other in a parade. First was Superstorm Sandy, which came ashore on Monday, October 29, with hurricane-force winds and heavy surf. A week later, a powerful nor'easter rolled in on Election Day. The latter storm hit Ellisville with more raw violence than had Sandy and instantly formed a new barrier spit that partially blocked the Ellisville inlet and began restricting tidal flows into and out of the marsh. It is this type of tidal blockage that the Friends group works to prevent, and to alleviate when it occurs, so as to maintain a tidal range conducive for the full recovery of native marsh plants and fisheries.

The Friends responded to the damage left behind by these storms with several days of inlet maintenance work in early January, again contracting with Brian Richmond. Richmond and his sons quickly reopened the blocked inlet and repaired the berm that serves as the south channel wall, straightening the channel to enable self-scouring when sediment gets washed in by the tides. The work began on January 7 and was completed in three days.

Not to be denied, nature struck again on February 8 in the form of Winter Storm Nemo (also known as the Blizzard of 2013). This was a mighty, long-duration storm that rivaled the so-called "Perfect Storm," or the No-Name Storm, of 1991. Enormous waves driven by powerful, northeasterly gale-force winds overpowered the rock jetty at Ellisville Harbor State Park and poured millions of gallons of sand-laced water over and into the channel.

The sand and cobble berm that had held the Ellisville channel in place never stood a chance. Overnight, a huge barrier spit formed, instantly reaching as high as six feet above mean high water and one hundred yards wide in places. Within days, water began to back up in the marsh as the newly formed spit prevented it from emptying completely at low tide. Within a few successive tide cycles, the new spit quickly extended to a length of five hundred feet.

Funded by an emergency corporate grant and armed with a one-time emergency waiver of the time-of-year permit restriction by MassDEP, work to rebreach the barrier spit and repair the south channel berm began on Monday, March 4, and was completed by that Wednesday, again fully restoring tidal flows to the marsh. However, midway through the work it became apparent that a storm forecast to pass south of New England was going to strike at least a glancing blow to Massachusetts.

The third nor'easter smashed into the Massachusetts coast, destroying homes, eroding bluffs, and leaving coastal devastation in its wake. As a result, the winter's repeated efforts to maintain unrestricted tidal flows to the marsh were unsuccessful. A barrier spit remained in place, albeit smaller in size than it might have been, and the channel remained bent, which would need to be addressed the following winter.

The Friends' timely interventions undoubtedly lessened the severity of the inlet blockage. It is entirely possible that a barrier spit of one thousand feet or more in length would have existed throughout that summer and fall if the spit had not been breached twice. A spit of that size had already been shown by hydrodynamic modeling to have a negative impact on Ellisville Marsh's vegetation and water quality.[2] Similar patterns of winter storms and barrier spit formation were seen in subsequent years as climate conditions changed.

Unfortunately, the Friends were not always able to move as nimbly when conditions at the inlet changed dynamically. The organization's board ordinarily acts to restore efficient tidal flows under its local, state, and federal regulatory permits. However, given delayed action by the US Army Corps of Engineers on a new federal permit in 2016 and the fact that it contained new conditions and requirements, the Friends leadership decided to avoid any risk of possible noncompliance and deferred that year's planned maintenance event. The contract with Brian Richmond was canceled. This effectively closed the door on inlet work in 2016 given that the maintenance window was September through March (with the TOY waiver from the MassDEP).

Lessons Learned

Several painful lessons were learned in those early years. The Friends would need to argue for extension of the annual dredging window from January 31 to March 31 every year to minimize the odds that January inlet work would be nullified by late-winter storms. The winter of 2012–13 highlighted the risk inherent in reopening the inlet in January.

A more permanent, long-term solution would also be needed to counter what appeared to be an emerging pattern of increasingly severe storms if the inlet was to be kept open. The Friends initiated discussions with the commonwealth about this course of action. While two past secretaries of environmental affairs had stated formally and publicly that the long-term solution was mainly the commonwealth's responsibility, no concrete steps had been taken to plan, design, or implement one.

The state park rock jetty, it was already known, is a major

culprit contributing to the periodic blockage of the Ellisville Inlet. The process by which it does so is well understood. The rock structure stores copious amounts of sand on its north side, much of which is pushed over the jetty and into the channel when nor'easters hit. Consideration of its role in inlet blockage and how to mitigate these effects would have to be part of the discussion with the state.

A berm made entirely of sand, to which the Friends were limited under its permits, does not stop storms like those that came ashore in 2012–13 from diverting the inlet. Serious investigation into more sustainable alternatives was needed. The Friends believed it was time to consider approaches that had been tested and proven elsewhere, especially those that are naturally sustainable, including nature-based approaches known as "living shoreline" solutions. Periodic inlet maintenance, although helpful in maintaining tidal flows to the salt marsh, was only a short-term measure, a stopgap.

The Winter of 2018

Every year by mid-February, the board of directors must decide whether to conduct inlet maintenance—2018 was no different. Each maintenance event costs thousands of dollars and requires a significant time commitment by board members, all of whom have competing priorities for their time. The main question that must be answered is always the same: Have winter storms formed a barrier spit long and high enough that tidal flows into and out of the marsh have become restricted?

The Blizzard of 2018 hit the coastline with a massive wallop in early January. Thousands of cubic yards of sand were cascaded over the rock jetty on the state park side of the inlet by what amounted to a seventeen-foot-high tide, in a place where twelve feet is typically the highest level of the year. It seemed inevitable that this would trigger maintenance work in March. The Friends' request to waive the time-of-year restriction, which had been granted by the MassDEP in December, allowed work to be scheduled until March 31 rather than January 31.

However, careful analysis of the barrier spit in February and its likely impact on the marsh ecosystem led the board to defer maintenance until the following winter. Ellen Russell, the board's scientific adviser, observed, "The height of the berm appears less than I remember it in the past and does not seem as likely to cause blockage. The curve the channel is taking is par for the course and also does not seem to be threatening down coast."[3]

In fact, the behavior of the barrier spit has changed in recent years. At times, it recedes and migrates back northward. The process by which this happens is not yet understood, but there is hope that the inlet may be seeking a more stable profile that extends the time between maintenance events.

A couple more storms occurred in 2018, after which it was too late to take the necessary steps to enable the work in March. A final major storm was unleashed in early April, a punctuation mark for the winter just ending. It was one more indication that a pattern shift was under way. Winter storms are likely to increase in frequency and power. An entry in the Friends' newsletter in 2018 reinforces this theme: "Names to remember: Grayson, Riley, Quinn, Skylar. Massive winter storms exploded hundreds of miles offshore and pummeled the Massachusetts coastline, producing historic flooding and coastal erosion as many as five times . . . . Sea water that flooded in with super-high tides became trapped and unable to ebb due to storm surge and wind-driven surf. The storms repeatedly overwhelmed the state park rock jetty and carried large volumes of pent-up sand into the Ellisville inlet, spawning a new barrier spit and diverting the flow. Coastal bluffs were battered up and down the Gulf of Maine. For this year at least, March became the new January."[4]

Restoring the Flow

The reader may have noticed continuing use of the words "inlet maintenance" in place of "dredging," the word commonly reflected in the project's regulatory permits. Why is this? "Dredging" does not accurately describe what the Friends do. In fact, most members of the Friends' board cringe when they hear this word. They are, first and foremost, environmentally attuned, and the word assaults their sensibilities.

Environmental regulators, some of whom have never been to the Ellisville project site, might imagine dredging as an operation with barges and excavators making deep gouges in a navigation channel or improving a harbor. They have been conditioned to think this way—most permitted dredging projects involve months of work. What the Friends do, by comparison, is so light-handed that it does not merit being called dredging. The work typically involves two days of an excavator creating a twenty-foot-wide cut through a ten-foot-high sand spit to allow a stream to flow through it. All the work is performed from dry land.

Heavy equipment is required, albeit only for a few days. Any environmental impact that might be associated with the use of this equipment is along the route the machines travel to the barrier spit. The potential for harm is lessened once they get to the work site, because it is mostly under water at high tide and largely devoid of vegetation.

Volunteers carefully plan the route and cordon off natural resource areas such as incipient patches of *S. alterniflora* that have begun to take hold along the channel. The Friends' experienced shorebird-monitoring team scouts the route ahead of time for threatened shorebirds that may have returned early for the nesting season.

On the chosen day, one can hear the machines coming from a distance. Unnatural sounds. Metallic screams and groans. Two yellow hulks come into view as they round Al Marsh's old dredge mound and rumble along the channel toward the spit.

But once the big machines are in place, something miraculous happens. Their long arms swing gracefully over the fresh cut they have made in the sand spit. Jason Richmond and his brother Brian sweep the excavators' buckets in a wide arc, then back again, countering each other's movements perfectly. They become partners in a rhythmic ballet—a somehow elegant pas de deux with ungainly dancers. Sand dribbles out of the buckets as the arms swing, making a fine, glistening shower that cascades onto a growing pyramid of sand.

The vibrations from the equipment surge through the winter air as they prepare to fully restore life-giving tidal flows to the salt marsh. One cannot help but marvel at the ease with which they move tons of blocking sand. They make quick work of a blockage that took a major storm to create and a multitude of daily tide cycles to extend and enlarge. They are ugly to look at and their sounds assail our ears, yet the machines are impressive for the raw power they bring to the task at hand.

Excavation of the new channel path begins at the edge of the bay and gradually proceeds landward. Two excavators work in tandem in years when the barrier spit is large, ten feet or more in height. They pull bucket after bucket of sand from a trench that grows wider and deeper by the hour, emptying their buckets onto a rising pyramid of sand. A front-end loader will push this sand into the diverted channel to block it once the straight-channel path has been restored.

Initially, the trench is dry at the bottom, but as the hours wear on, water creeps in as the tide begins to turn. All the stockpiled sand must be stored safely above the high-tide line to avoid having it wash away. Work stops for the day after just a few hours. The tide is rising. In Ellisville, there is typically a ten-foot height difference between low and high tide. During the date window chosen by the Friends to perform inlet maintenance, the tidal range can be close to fourteen feet.

The inlet maintenance experience of 2019 was fairly typical. It had been four years since the Friends last opened the partially blocked Ellisville Marsh inlet. The barrier spit had grown to nearly one thousand feet in length, and water had become bottled up in the marsh, unable to drain before the tide turned and started coming in again. This ponding effect impacted water quality, vegetation, fisheries, and wildlife. All that changed the week of March 25 when Brian Richmond and his sons breached the barrier spit and restored the channel to its desired position as shown on the local, state, and federal permits. A massive pile of sediment was created in the process (the Great Pyramid of Ellisville, to some observers) to block the existing channel bed and avoid the possibility of dual inlets. Unrestricted tidal flows would soon be restored.

The second day of work is worth witnessing. Brian Richmond's sons have by now cut an impressive trench, twenty feet wide and slightly deeper than the mean low-water level to ensure a strong, natural flow once the inlet is fully reopened. The trench runs from the edge of Cape Cod Bay to the last remnant of the barrier spit standing between the trench and the pent-up water, a ten-foot-thick dam of packed sand. This remnant holds back the water that has pooled at the elbow of the channel. The inlet is not technically closed because it still has an outlet to the sea, although it is bent at a right angle. Nevertheless, there is a lot of water held back here, waiting to be set free.

What happens next is carefully choreographed. A front-end loader begins pushing the massive pyramid of stockpiled sand from its resting place on the spit into the existing channel at the point where it bends sharply to the south. This blocks the flow and starts to build back pressure behind the dam. At the same time, the excavator reaches out to its fullest extension and grabs huge buckets of sand out of the dam wall. Within minutes the dam is breached and water bursts through the gap. As the loader blocks more and more of the diverted channel and the pressure of the water still left in the marsh builds, hundreds of thousands of gallons rush through the gap, completing the job.

The water has nowhere to go but through the new opening,

and it dashes to the sea. Its rip current is easily visible a quarter-mile out in the bay. One could surf on the standing waves it generates. Gulls gather in a screaming frenzy above the froth as minnows and other edibles are caught up and swept out into the bay.

For those who have watched the inlet blockage worsen with each tide cycle and waited patiently for the opportunity to restore the direct-channel connection between salt marsh and sea, this is a dramatic and joyful moment. It is the fireworks finale on the Fourth of July. The moment of breach should be set to stirring music. Wagner, perhaps.

Comprehending the Inlet

Of all the people who are actively involved in the Friends' project, Jack Scambos is the most intrigued by the workings of the Ellisville Marsh inlet. He has, among other good qualities, a keen engineering mind and is by his nature driven to decode and understand complex systems. His day job involves helping Fortune 500 companies recover oil from contaminated water and reduce water consumption.

When Scambos is at his family home in Ellisville, he scrutinizes the inlet, strives to understand intuitively how it functions, and works to decode the mechanics of how natural forces operate on the marsh inlet. He pays close attention to what happens whenever the inlet is reopened, always looking for better ways to configure the channel and sequence the reopening work to extend the length of time before maintenance is needed again.

Scambos has taken the time to discuss the inlet with the old-timers, especially Al Marsh, which enables him to understand what they did to maintain access to the old harbor for their lobster boats. The recurrent theme that emerged from these conversations was "straight, deep, and narrow," referring to the most efficient channel configuration. Scambos hammers away at this during permitting discussions and when he meets with Brian Richmond to sequence the inlet maintenance work.

Straight, deep, and narrow is the channel configuration that directs the ebb flow of water coming from the marsh most powerfully, scouring out accumulated sand, seaweed, algae, and other buildup in the channel that might otherwise begin to form a blockage of the inlet. Draining a salt marsh is like draining a bathtub. Pull the plug and the water races out. A straight path works best.

Whenever the discussion turns to how the Friends and its contractor should perform inlet maintenance and re-create the most sustainable inlet profile, Scambos weighs in. The Friends' actions reflect his deep understanding of the inlet's natural dynamics acquired over the years, always staying within the parameters of the approved permit plans. Narrowing the channel within the approved plan width is allowable. One can do less than what is shown, but never more.

No matter what expertise and knowledge the Friends have acquired about the workings of the Ellisville Marsh inlet, believing that any of us is in a position to exert control is utterly foolish. Nature always has the last say. Within a few tide cycles of maintenance work being completed and the inlet restored, nature begins to resculpt the new channel, smoothing the edges with hundreds of millions of gallons of water.

The marsh drains fully within a couple of hours after being straightened. An odor like rotten eggs may hang in the air for several days—this is a good sign. It means the water level in the marsh is dropping lower than before, low enough to expose the marsh's benthic layer of decomposing material to the air again.

The equipment is gone. Peace and quiet has returned to Ellisville Marsh. The marsh is breathing easily now. But there is much more work to be done. Monitoring the health of the marsh ecosystem once again becomes the focus of attention.

CHAPTER 8

The Closer You Look

THERE ARE A GREAT many ways to diagnose a patient. We can be x-rayed, scanned, and probed. Our heart rate, blood pressure, and temperature can be monitored. Our blood can be tested for all manner of things. So too can the health of a seventy-acre salt marsh be assessed.

We can peer down at this complex, living system from above using advanced imaging technology. We can surveil the landscape on foot and in boats with binoculars and spotting scopes. We can put the tiniest, unlikeliest things we find under a microscope. Using a variety of tools, we can assemble a detailed, composite picture of this natural place. When we do, we marvel at not having been able to see it before in its rich totality.

And when symptoms appear, such as the disappearance of acres of saltmarsh cordgrass, we come to realize something is wrong. It is our job to address the underlying cause before it is too late. Otherwise the patient might die, and it will have been on our watch.

The Friends' arduous journey through the permitting process created stringent conditions for the performance of work to reopen the blocked inlet. The permits came with a twenty-page attachment describing nine environmental monitoring programs the Friends had agreed to undertake and maintain as a condition of permit issuance. Volunteer teams continue to conduct most of these programs more than a decade later and have collected a large amount of environmental data that can be used to assess the health of the marsh and its interconnected ecosystems.

Data are submitted in electronic format to a host of local, state, and federal agencies every December. However, environmental monitoring and data collection to satisfy permit conditions are only part of the story. Identifying the factors that contribute to a healthy salt marsh or detract from it is the main goal. At Ellisville Marsh, it is not enough to simply observe the effect of salt marsh die-off and attribute it to periodic, sustained inlet closures.

A correlation between inlet closure and marsh health, no matter how weak or strong the apparent relationship may be, does not prove the former to be the cause of the latter, especially in a complex, natural system where many other factors come into play. So this revitalization project faced several scientific challenges moving forward. Most of these were reflected as requirements in the project's regulatory permits:

- Detect and measure changes over time in wetlands resources and coastal patterns.

- Monitor the current health of the marsh's wetland system, and judge how its underlying natural processes are functioning.

- Closely monitor and protect (mainly from other humans) sensitive wetland and coastal resources, especially threatened and endangered species.

- Pursue a sustainable, long-term solution to the underlying problems that cause marsh decline.

The Friends believe that the on-again, off-again pattern of marsh inlet blockage is a causal factor that helps explain Ellisville Marsh die-off. Maintaining unrestricted tidal flows was therefore expected to help restore equilibrium within the marsh system. To verify this, the Friends agreed to undertake multiple, environmental monitoring and data collection programs as part of the project. These programs generally fell into one of the four general areas listed above.

Tracking changes in the marsh, on the barrier beach, and offshore over the years is an important aspect of the Friends' environmental monitoring. The organization's programs record conditions both inside and outside the marsh as time-series data. These data hold the potential to identify factors that contribute to declining marsh health and track how conditions have changed from a baseline.

Critical data collection and monitoring requirements imposed as permit conditions included the following:

- Piping Plover nest monitoring and protection
- Beach elevation measurements
- Hydrodynamic modeling to determine tidal range
- Water quality sampling
- Offshore eelgrass monitoring
- Shellfish survey work
- Wetlands vegetation monitoring
- Finfish monitoring via reporting of catches by fishermen and -women
- Photographic analysis of the barrier spit

These monitoring programs are quite labor intensive. Anyone who happens to be nearby on a day in the summer over ninety degrees might notice a person standing in the middle of the salt marsh. In the early years, chances are it was Ellen Russell, working on her doctoral thesis, identifying factors that influence the health of wetland vegetation in the salt marsh. She supervised the installation of piezometers (one-inch-diameter screened PVC pipe) at ninety-seven locations throughout the marsh. Her initial team of volunteer recruits and, later on, college student interns would then identify the types of vegetation present in a one-meter-square plot surrounding each piezometer and estimate the percentage cover using standard survey techniques.

Multiple water quality monitoring rounds were conducted at eight locations in the marsh, channel, freshwater inputs, and ocean front, looking at temperature, dissolved oxygen, conductivity, chlorophyll, salinity, total dissolved solids, pH, and turbidity.[1] Three stilling wells were built to house pressure data loggers (tidal gauges) and sunk into the marsh, channel, and ocean at fixed depths in order to record the variation in tidal range between these locations. Tidal data are downloaded in late summer, and GPS data points are maintained for all plots, sampling, and stilling well locations so that the Friends may return to these exact locations in subsequent monitoring years.

Estimating Plant Coverage

One of the most important of the monitoring programs focuses on the extent and condition of *S. alterniflora* and other wetlands plants. Ellen Russell's vegetation monitoring plots are revisited each summer by the Friends' summer intern. Within each plot the percentage coverage by each of the various plants is estimated. The data that emerge from this annual exercise indicate the extent and density of not just *S. alterniflora* but also some sixteen other wetland plants.

Counting plants in a seventy-acre salt marsh in the summer is difficult and tedious work. The Friends' environmental monitoring intern can often be seen crouching in the middle of the marsh under a blazing sun and in high humidity while gathering the necessary data. It can be dangerous work. Some areas of the marsh contain a kind of hydraulic mud that behaves like quicksand: step into it and down you go, and better hope the tide is not coming in.

An incident a few years back exemplifies the risk. On one particularly hot day, two women decided to make a beeline across Ellisville Marsh on the return to their car. One of the women became stuck in the mud and was unable to extricate herself. She began sinking. The other called 911. It took a ladder truck from the Plymouth Fire Department with its ladder extended horizontally over the marsh to reach the woman. A TV news crew arrived in time to see the firefighters hosing the rescued woman down to clean the mud off her. A powerful, rotten-egg smell permeated the air around her. Lesson: Never try walking across a salt marsh at low tide.

A Tiny Discovery

Many discoveries have been made during the Friends' journey, some more remarkable than others. During her 2010 vegetation survey, before the Friends began bringing on college students as summer interns, Russell noticed a white scale on the stems of many of the *S. alterniflora* plants. She took samples back to the lab at the University of Massachusetts (UMass), where she was completing her doctoral degree in plant biology.

After determining that the white coating was not salt crystals in the way any determined scientist would, by licking it, Russell showed the coating to a UMass colleague, who identified it as *Haliaspis spartinae*, a tiny parasitic insect that appears as clusters of small white fibrous deposits or scales.

But there was more. Serendipitously, Dr. George Japoshvili, a professor from the University of Georgia in Eastern Europe, was visiting at the time. He was able to coax a microscopic bug out of the scale. It was unlike any other. A new species of insect had been discovered—a tiny, parasitic wasp. It was to be called *Encarsia ellisvillensis*.[2] The more closely you look, the more you notice. Russell summarizes the discovery and what it tells us about life in the marsh beyond plain view:

> *Encarsia ellisvillensis* is a newly identified species of wasp recently found in Ellisville Marsh. . . . [The wasp] is not quite nano-scale in size and has a parasitic relationship with its host, *Haliaspis spartinae*, a fairly common insect living on salt marsh grass. *Haliaspis spartinae* . . . appears as clusters of small white fibrous deposits or "scales" (hence its common name—scale), on the upper surfaces

of *Spartina alterniflora* leaves. It is related to some of the more common scale insects that are considered pests of fruit and ornamental trees. Found in infestation levels in marshes that experience hydraulic stress, it often coats the plants' lower leaves, blocking sunlight and sucking nutrients, and causing the plants' eventual decline. . . .

Salt marsh vegetation has low plant species diversity as only about fifteen plant species regularly occupy a typical salt marsh. Salt marshes, by virtue of high salinities, low oxygen in the "soils," and periodic inundations are quite hostile places for plant growth. We know, however, that below the vegetation canopy, there are many regular inhabitants and visitors that find the marsh optimal for breeding, rearing of young, living, and dying. Those are just the things we see—who would have guessed that this complex struggle between host (*Spartina alterniflora*), prey (*Haliaspsis spartinae*), and parasite (*Encarsia ellisvillensis*) has been going on, virtually invisible to our eyes! So, the next time you gaze at the seemingly monoculture stands of soothing green and yellow salt marsh grass, imagine what goes on within![3]

Photographic Images

Most of the work monitoring the health of Ellisville Marsh takes place on the ground. Aerial photogrammetry, however, relies on a high-resolution, infrared camera in an aircraft flying over the marsh at low altitude to create orthophotos—three-dimensional images. The photographs can be used to locate objects of interest by latitude, longitude, and elevation relative to mean sea level. Healthy plants give off heat, which the infrared camera picks up. Areas that appear more reddish in color tend to have healthier plants. Cooler areas appear as gray, indicating less healthy or dormant vegetation, so the time of year is important.

Aerial infrared orthophotos can be calibrated to on-the-ground conditions, such as the plant coverage data collected each summer at Ellisville Marsh, to enhance the accuracy of GIS photographic interpretation. Infrared images taken periodically by the Town of Plymouth, along with those commissioned by the Friends, tell the marsh's recent story and help connect the dots regarding the role of inlet blockage in the health of wetland vegetation.

The first such orthophoto was taken for the Friends by Col-East in August 2008. Each photo is referenced to a series of ground control points whose exact location and elevation are known and provides insights into the health as well as extent of coverage of vegetation. Since the orthophotos are rendered to identical scale and reference points, they can be compared to determine how wetlands vegetation and water flows have changed in the intervening years, reflecting both the impacts of dredging of the inlet and other factors such as storms and natural movements of sediment. Together with Ellen Russell's on-the-ground analysis using the remaining vegetation sampling plots, scientific conclusions are more likely to be formed.

By the time of the 2018 aerial orthophotos, the technology had gone fully digital. Film had been phased out, and the cost had risen. Astute Ellisville residents might have noticed a white aircraft with red stripes flying over the marsh the morning of August 16 at dead low tide. The plane was in the process of capturing the highest-resolution photograph ever taken of Ellisville Marsh and its immediate surroundings, equipped with digital camera equipment capable of capturing both infrared (IR) and red-green-blue (RGB) bands of light. Infrared imagery records heat given off by plant life and is therefore useful in determining the health of marsh vegetation. Red-green-blue uses the primary colors to produce an image that more closely matches the human perception of color, sometimes referred to as "true color."

The latest images are larger in size than what can be created by any camera you own, "weighing in" at 1,300 megabytes. This was the third in a series of orthophotos (also taken in 2008 and 2011) the Friends have commissioned, making Ellisville Marsh one of the most closely studied natural resources in the commonwealth. Analysis of the new image was overseen by Ellen Russell, with assistance from her colleagues at the University of Massachusetts–Amherst.

This kind of investigation, with its high-tech tools and scientific deductions, brings to mind television programs like *CSI: Crime Scene Investigation* with its whizbang science labs and chasing of clues by determined scientists. What the Friends do feels a little like that at times. One can zoom into the digital image with special software and see an object the size of a half dollar lying on the ground, a remarkable thing considering the camera is carried on an airplane three thousand feet up.

Aerial orthophotos are not cheap or easy to obtain however. Each one can cost upward of $2,000. Weather and atmospheric conditions limit when photos can be taken. The resulting pictures must be viewed with special software owing to their size, and most home computers lack the memory to load them. But once the images are in scientists' hands, each one is found to be loaded with highly detailed information describing physical conditions in the salt marsh.

Detecting and monitoring changes beyond the salt marsh itself, along the barrier beach and spit as well as just offshore in the bay, requires different approaches. Photographs are taken on a monthly basis from a fixed location on top of the coastal bank just south of the inlet. Looking down on the beachscape and inlet from a relatively high angle, continuously over a fifteen-year period, one can see objectively how the coastline is physically changing. And by using fixed reference points such as a boulder the locals call harbor rock and a rock groin farther up the state park beach, photographs taken years apart can be scaled and overlaid for direct comparison.

Thanks in part to on-site training the Friends received from Malcolm MacGregor, the Friends are able to apply GPS technology in a variety of ways that support their environmental monitoring programs. Using one of the simplest and lowest-cost handheld GPS devices available, volunteers have located the positions of the tidal gauges that are placed in the marsh, channel, and ocean every summer. Volunteers also map the offshore eelgrass bed with GPS once a year. And GPS locations accurate to within a few feet for the beach and marsh transects are used for survey work. Mapping the edges of the inlet channel to the bay at low tide with the GPS unit, for example, produces an especially valuable record considering how dynamically the beach and tidal flats can change within a matter of weeks.

Photographs can also document long-term changes. One photographic comparison showed that the intertidal zone at Ellisville Beach, the area covered by water at high tide and uncovered at low tide, had dropped three or four feet in the space of ten years because of ocean scouring. But one did not necessarily need scientific monitoring to determine this. An old, rusted sailboat swing keel weighing several hundred pounds has resurfaced after being buried for decades.

Photographic comparisons also enabled the Friends to measure how far the grass dune line has retreated on the state park side of the marsh channel—a hundred feet or more in the past decade. These are dramatic changes in the coastal landscape over a relatively short period of time. Ten years is the blink of an eye in the life of a coastal resource.

Low-Tech Measuring of Beach Elevations

Changes in the beachscape can be measured another way, using a device known as an Emery rod.[4] This low-tech, hands-on measuring technique is seemingly old-fashioned. Emery rods are a physical manifestation of a parallelogram. This wooden contraption resembles an oversize parallel ruler, the device navigators use to move a line of bearing on a navigational chart to the compass rose to determine its precise direction in degrees relative to north.

The Emery rods are comprised of two vertical sticks spaced

five feet apart and connected by a pair of horizontal crosspieces on swivels. The first set was donated to the Friends by staff persons at the Massachusetts Office of Coastal Zone Management. The Friends fabricated a second set so two teams could work at the same time.

Volunteers Marc and Lisa Colburn joined former Friends director Kelley O'Neel and Mary Ellen Mastrorilli on the team that recorded changes in beach elevations in seven Ellisville locations, twice per year. These measurements enabled the Friends to accurately document buildup and removal of sand that results from wind, tides, and water flows in the vicinity of the salt marsh inlet without having to retain a survey team. The first measurements were taken in May 2007, prior to the start of nesting by threatened shorebirds, which can block access to parts of the beach for up to several months. With four team members, each measurement cycle was typically completed in a single day.

The Friends' beach measurement teams systematically worked their way down the beach along the straight-line transects, stopping every five feet to measure how many centimeters higher or lower the beach has sloped at that point. The result is a detailed representation of how a vertical slice, or section, of the beach would look from the dune to the low-water mark.

Some of the beach transects were five hundred feet long as the sand and cobble bars extend far out at low tide. The transect data are invaluable for understanding how the barrier spit, barrier beach, and shoreline gain or lose height over time. They show where sand has piled up and where it has been worn down by tides and weather.

Because of the proliferation of poison ivy in the dune grass, not to mention ticks that could cause Lyme disease and other illnesses, O'Neel and Mastrorilli came dressed in white clothing with long sleeves and tucked-in pants with their hair snugged down under their caps. The getups resembled hazmat suits. Their twice-per-summer data-gathering routine prompted bewildered stares from beachgoers. Has there been a toxic chemical spill?

Are they from the nuclear plant? No, they were simply measuring the ups and downs in the beach.

Mapping the Offshore Eelgrass Bed

Measuring the extent of the offshore eelgrass bed, mentioned earlier in our discussion of regulatory requirements, is similarly hands-on. Two volunteers in a kayak—one to spot the grass below the surface and paddle, the other to enter GPS data points—move along the outside edge of the eelgrass bed during dead low tide in calm water conditions. A handheld GPS device records the latitude and longitude of the bed's edge points to within about six feet.

It happens in the early morning when conditions on the water are typically calm. Early risers might notice two people in a bright yellow kayak paddling around slowly off Ellisville beach around 7:00 a.m. The ocean kayak is on loan to the Friends from Vlad and Marie Hruby. Measurements are taken during a seasonally low tide, often coinciding with a full moon.

This work can be therapeutic. The kayak floats along on a glassy surface with the paddler peering down through crystal clear water at shimmery green plant stalks. The reverie is interrupted only by the clicking of the handheld GPS device, six hundred to seven hundred times during the hour-long circumnavigation of the bed. The volunteers almost become part of the offshore ecosystem. After a decade of marsh inlet maintenance, the bed appears remarkably stable. In years when the inlet migrated, "dents" in the eelgrass bed have been observed. These data suggest that maintaining the inlet in a stable location is probably beneficial.

Although the programs described thus far are aimed at constructing a picture of how the marsh and its immediate surroundings change over time, significant attention is also paid to monitoring the current condition of wetland resources and how natural processes are functioning. Key among these is measurement of the actual tidal range in the marsh: how high the water rises and how low it falls when the tides come and go.

Tidal range in the salt marsh is at the heart of the issue—to what extent does periodic blockage of the marsh inlet constrain tidal elevation, the vertical difference between low and high water levels? As mentioned, key marsh indicator plants thrive in a fairly narrow set of conditions. Too much waterlogging and they die, as experience at Ellisville Marsh bears out. How does one measure tidal heights and troughs? Indirectly, by measuring barometric pressure.

Pressure gauges called HOBO data loggers are submerged and fixed in place in several locations in the salt marsh, marsh channel, and offshore to record hourly the relative barometric pressure at each spot over the time span of a month.[5] When barometric air pressure data are also collected, water levels can be derived from the recorded pressure differences. Filling higher and draining lower is the goal for healthy *S. alterniflora* and a host of other plants that inhabit the low marsh.

Water quality and salinity have also been sampled during the summer months over many years. Salinity, as the state's aforementioned 2007 study of salt marshes indicated, is important to the health of key salt marsh plant species. And as we know, Ellisville Marsh receives freshwater as well as saltwater flows. A delicate balance must be maintained between the two for native vegetation to flourish.

Shellfish and Finfish

Shellfish and finfish were also supposed to be counted. Indeed, the Friends' stated objective in keeping the salt marsh inlet open is to revitalize fisheries and wildlife. However, the number of clams and fish present proved difficult to measure. Regulatory requirements spelled out exactly where the Friends were to conduct sample surveys for shellfish, that is, along a transect that crossed the main channel on the old harbor.

Almost no shellfish were found where the Friends were told to look. However, fifty yards away in a large sandbar one could see hundreds of vent holes made by soft-shelled clams. This survey requirement amounted to another wasted expense for an outside consultant, twice incurred by the Friends, when simple observation should have sufficed. If those specifying the shellfish monitoring requirements had visited the site, perhaps they could have avoided the folly of setting the survey transects where no clams would be found.

What about finfish? Plenty of striped bass and other fish enter the marsh to feed when the tide comes in. There is a veritable buffet of minnows, baitfish, and tiny, delectable crustaceans called grass shrimp in the marsh, so many in fact that frustrated fishermen standing on the rock jetty at the marsh inlet know that stripers are not in the least bit hungry when they swim back out of the salt marsh with the ebbing tide.

One of the Friends' programs involved asking fishermen and -women to report their catches using an online tool created to collect anecdotal data on finfish prevalence. Who would know better what fish are present than one who fishes there? But secrecy is paramount in these circles. One does not disclose locations where fish are present. There is an inverse correlation here: the greater the number of fish present, the less likely the cooperation.

Notwithstanding explanations of how fish counts could inform the Friends' work to revitalize fisheries in the marsh, saltwater anglers remained suspicious of the organization's motives. Both the shellfish and finfish data gathering requirements were waived after the first few years when the fruitlessness of such programs had become apparent to everyone.

Opportunities for monitoring fisheries, wildlife, and vegetation appear from variety of sources. The Friends take advantage of these to better understand the totality of the intertwined ecosystems that exist around Ellisville Marsh. Great white sharks previously tagged on Cape Cod are tracked at several locations in Cape Cod Bay, for example. Ellisville is one of these locations. A bright-yellow, cylindrical buoy marked CB-1 (CB reportedly stands for "clever buoy") is anchored a quarter mile off Ellisville Harbor State Park. When a tagged shark swims within two hundred yards it records a "ping." Unfortunately for swimmers and kayakers in the area, the buoy does not issue alerts in real time. The shark data it collects are downloaded only once or twice a year. Only then do we learn that sharks have come by. We also learn the nicknames they have been given, like Margaret and Jameson.

Close monitoring of environmental conditions at Ellisville Marsh over more than a decade and scientific modeling have provided a wealth of scientific data and significant insights into the health of the marsh. Little doubt exists that salt marsh die-off is strongly influenced by excessive inundation when the inlet is even partially blocked. More rapid changes can be expected as sea level rises and ocean temperatures warm. Notwithstanding any of this, some of the Friends' monitoring programs turned out to be much more instructive than others. In particular, monitoring a species of small shorebirds taught us how fragile life can be where land meets sea.

CHAPTER 9
....
Invisible Birds

⌒

THEY ARE HERE, BUT you cannot see them. Invisible against the backdrop of beach sand and scattered stones, dressed in a camouflage suit of buff-colored feathers and fluff. Their black neckband and forehead hardly give them away. Nor does their tiny orange-and-black bill. Hours of experience have taught that finding them requires patience and heightened awareness. Stop walking. Look for the slightest of movements. Listen for the tell-tale peeping carried on the wind. Take a deep breath. Let yourself be absorbed into the landscape so completely that you become no more than a solitary figure watching a film in an empty theater. Let the stillness engulf you and wash away thoughts. Become aware of everything that surrounds you. And then, you see the pair of them. They are standing patiently not ten feet away, looking up at you, wondering why you have set foot into their world.

One has to marvel at the pluck of the diminutive Piping Plover. She and her mate arrive, like clockwork and without fanfare, in March or April to stake out their nesting territory amid the sand and scattered cobble of Ellisville Beach. One may have arrived a few weeks early, patiently waiting for a mate. They have flown a thousand miles or more from their wintering grounds in Florida or the Bahamas. The beachscape as they knew it from the last nesting season has been rearranged by winter storms. No visual references have survived. Every trace of what was then familiar has disappeared. Yet they return to the same place on the same beach.

Winter storms delayed the start of nesting in 2015, but several pairs had already returned by April. Birds the Friends had gotten to know in prior years were tracked to other beaches. One of the Ellisville plovers (Waldo, a banded bird) had been reported on a beach in North Carolina just a few weeks earlier and subsequently nested on Sagamore Beach, just down the coast. The following year, three plovers were spotted on Ellisville Beach in mid-March by Brad Winn and Paula Marcoux, one of the earliest sightings of these shorebirds here. More evidence of climate change perhaps? Winn captured a stunning photo of one of the plovers. Could it be Muttonchops, the diligent parent who shepherded his three chicks around the beach for four weeks the prior summer until they fledged? The distinctive neck band suggested the possibility.

The prior year's birds sometimes return to within a few feet of their old nest, a shallow depression scraped in the sand that held four eggs, now long gone. Volunteers remember the nests as clearly as the birds might. Sometimes it seems we can approach a pair without arousing fear. Or is it our imagination playing tricks? Do they cue on the binoculars hanging around our necks or the deliberate, stop-and-go cadence of our walk? We must not seem to pose an overt threat. We are outsiders to their world, but they seem willing to tolerate us.

For many beachgoers, the first exposure to threatened shorebirds like Piping Plovers and Least Terns is the fencing. One may arrive at the shore ready to sunbathe, swim, or fish only to be confronted by a large swath of beachfront fenced off by wooden posts and fraying orange twine. Signs indicate that the area is closed to protect nesting shorebirds and that stiff penalties can be imposed for noncompliance.[1] They tell us that federal and state Endangered Species Acts dictate the extent of such protection, even on private property. The fencing irks some people. In Plymouth, one occasionally sees outward expressions of this: a bumper sticker that reads "Piping Plover tastes like chicken" or wanton vandalism of fencing and signs.

Public agencies go to great lengths to protect these birds. The United States Fish and Wildlife Service (USFWS) brought legal action against the owners of public and private properties where feral cats threatened Piping Plover nests.[2] Not coincidentally, this agency played the key role in the Friends' decision to get into the Piping Plover protection business in the first place.

Early on in the Friends' discussions with federal and state agencies in preparation for submitting permit applications, a senior official within USFWS made it unmistakably clear that threatened species were the first, and in her view perhaps only, real consideration. The Friends would eventually come to realize that many of the agency people consider their individual mandates to be all that matters, a stance that ignores the highly intertwined nature of virtually all ecosystems. What if protecting Piping Plovers resulted in a net loss of some other valued natural resource?

The USFWS official indicated that permits might not be granted unless the Friends committed to funding a program to protect Piping Plovers throughout their nesting season, April to September. Such a program could cost as much as $10,000 annually. This was out of the question for a newly created and thinly funded nonprofit, so the Friends suggested instead that a volunteer program be established. There was some resistance to this idea among the parties present and clear reluctance on the part of USFWS to allow amateurs anywhere near nesting areas.

It was ultimately agreed that Friends volunteers would be trained and supervised by shorebird experts from Mass Audubon's Coastal Waterbird Program (CWP), which had by then been operating for twenty years. The program today protects nesting areas at 182 beaches along nearly 140 miles of Massachusetts coastline and manages the conservation of 30 to 40 percent of the state's Piping Plovers and 40 to 50 percent of Least Terns. It is one of the most highly respected entities working to protect coastal birds and barrier beaches in North America. Perhaps most impressive, CWP has trained and mentored more than fifteen hundred field staff and countless volunteers over the past thirty-five years, many of whom have gone on to careers in conservation science and environmental management.

The key to the Friends' startup shorebird nesting program was that Dr. Rebecca (Becky) Harris, CWP's director at the time, and Ellen Jedrey, assistant director, were open-minded and considered the Friends' program a potential partnership opportunity, perhaps even a means to leverage scarce resources. This is how the Friends got into the business of threatened shorebirds protection in 2007.

Within a few years, the Friends' monitoring team had earned the respect of USFWS and served as a model for how a volunteer-run monitoring program should function. Harris has said that she is unaware of any volunteer-led shorebird-monitoring program that has been as consistently reliable, devoted, and successful over the long term. And fifteen years later, the Friends are still partnering with Mass Audubon to protect shorebird nests and chicks on Ellisville Beach.

Perhaps most important, the program gave the Friends an understanding of where the plover pairs tend to nest on the beach. This knowledge is essential to plans for channel restoration and reuse of displaced sand for beach nourishment, which enhances shorebird nesting habitat. This knowledge also allows fencing to be deployed in areas where there is actual nesting activity, leaving more of the beach open for beachgoers.

The Threatened Shorebirds Monitoring Program

The earliest team of volunteers comprised four locals, several of whom became members of the Friends' board. There was Paula Marcoux, a food historian and backyard oven-builder of some repute, author of *Cooking with Fire*, and food editor of a South Shore magazine. Diane Jordan, a vigorous outdoorswoman, photographer, and landscaper, is a jack-of-all-trades hardy enough to stand duty for hours on end when inlet maintenance work is taking place in the coldest depths of New England winter. Bobbi Martino, for whom breathing salt air by the ocean is as essential as eating or sleeping. And me. With the possible exception of Marcoux, who knows something about everything natural, all of us were newcomers to the business of plover monitoring. The team had to start learning from square one.

The team was later joined by Henry Riter, an avid scuba diver; Christine Cody, a journalist and former naval officer; and Rosemary Smith, who protected plover chicks as if they were her own grandchildren. All of the trainees quickly succumbed to the small birds' charms. In the early days everything seemed remarkable—the birds' sometimes strange behavior, the creative spots they choose for nesting, discovery of a nest with eggs in it, the marvel of one-day-old chicks, and the emotional release that comes from watching a chick fledge fifty-plus days after incubation first began.

Team members brought a certain technological bias to organizing and managing the monitoring program that lay before them. Coordination was on a purely virtual basis from the beginning, with an online daily reporting log shared among team members to continuously build on what had been discovered about the birds' activities the day before. Heads-up emails often zipped between members of the team as remarkable events were observed. A graphic map of the beach was created from downloaded Google satellite images, which enabled team members to pinpoint for one another where nests had been located or were likely.

Face-to-face meetings were rare except when a team was needed to erect fencing. Because of this virtual approach, coordination of site visits and flows of information were continuously smooth and timely. This mode of operation turned out to be especially valuable when the COVID-19 pandemic hit in early 2020. It caused virtually no disruption to threatened shorebird monitoring.

Before explaining how this all worked and what was learned along the way, it is important to describe why there is a moral responsibility to this sort of undertaking. We humans are late-comers and, it can be argued, lower-importance users of the Ellisville Beach landscape. Plovers rely on the beach for essential nourishment and nesting habitat. Our uses, in comparison, are all discretionary, almost exclusively recreational these days. The beach is the Piping Plovers' world. They own it, though such may be a minority view among others who use the birds' beach habitats.

Plovers and terns have been in decline for over a hundred years, thanks in part to an earlier era in which the birds were hunted for their feathers to make fashionable ladies' hats and, perhaps more important for the tiny plovers, the encroachment of hard structures and coastal development on their shifting sand habitats. Following a rebound in the plover population that peaked around 1940, increased development and beach recreation in the postwar era caused a further population decline.

Only recently has the downward trend toward extinction of the species been reversed. Thanks to aggressive conservation measures, a total of only 135 nesting pairs of Piping Plovers in 1986 had recovered to 680 pairs by 2018, with CWP-managed sites accounting for about 15 percent of the Atlantic Coast population. By 2021, the number had recovered to 900. Yet nesting productivity remains under immense pressure, as Piping Plover habitat continues to be lost throughout the hemisphere, more toxins enter the atmosphere and water, and new predators appear on the scene. Add to this climate change and rampant overdevelopment of coastal areas.

Learning to Think Like a Plover

Working toward understanding what it must be like to *be* a Piping Plover is a necessary first step in helping reverse the decades-long trend toward extinction of their species. Gaining that appreciation takes time, as members of the Friends' all-volunteer monitoring team can attest. Learning about plovers, by closely observing them on a daily basis, is one of the most unusual and thought-provoking experiences most of the team ever had. Watching how plovers live and behave in their nesting habitat can be like visiting a foreign country.

On-the-job training has lasted fifteen years and counting. The most basic lesson team members learned from the outset, because CWP's trainers constantly emphasized and reemphasized it, is "First, do no harm." Team members learned how to avoid stepping on nests inadvertently and, just as important, how not to lead cunning predators to the prize.

Plovers' main protection from a host of predators is their natural camouflage coupled with instinctive behavior that allows them to virtually disappear into the beach landscape. So anyone tasked with protecting these birds must first learn how to find them. Harris and Jedrey, the team's mentors from CWP, were very patient. They taught us how to locate the birds' tracks so one could follow and deduce their activities. Tracks along the wrack line, the seaweed, and other material that marks high tide generally indicate feeding. Tracks leading up the beach from the water's edge can mean potential nesting activity.

Piping Plover tracks on a sandy beach are as indistinct as fresh snowflakes falling on bare ground. Their delicate imprint is made by three tiny toes. Delicate because it is left by something that weighs less than two ounces. Indistinct because the sand is constantly blowing around, absorbing water, or drying out. You mostly detect the faint track by turning toward the sun and looking down or looking back over where you have just walked if that is the direction of the sun. In any case, finding plover tracks is no easy feat, and trainees quickly attributed to their trainers extraordinary powers of observation.

"How the heck did they see that?" was often the unspoken thought about Harris and Jedrey. In hindsight, the better question would have been, "How did they *know it would be there*?" These two seasoned veterans of the plover trade had a sixth sense about where to find the birds on this unique stretch of beach that took members of the Friends' monitoring group time to acquire. Team members can now surmise where the birds will be without seeing or hearing them first.

Once in a while one comes across a strange-looking track that resembles a delicate chain stitch or straight-line zipper. The tiny footprints are close to each other in a tight, almost geometric pattern. This male behavior is a heads-up that serious business is about to take place or recently has—the male plover is "strutting his stuff."

And "strutting" is an apt description. The move is often referred to as "high stepping." The male stiffens his back to appear taller than he can possibly be and begins straight-leg, high-step marching. It is a bizarre yet captivating display, and one cannot help but laugh at his willingness to act so silly to get what he wants. Where did he learn that step? Does his strange behavior have the desired effect on the female?

The male's behavior does sometimes lead to mating, another strange affair. She stops in place. He vaults up and stands on her back. The image that comes to mind is the now-vintage photo of the space shuttle being carried back to Florida atop a Boeing 747 jumbo jet after a landing in the California desert.

Learning What to Look For

Understanding exactly what to look for is the next challenge. Piping Plover monitoring requires data gathering throughout the full nesting cycle: scraping, courtship, mating, egg laying, incubation, hatching, growth, and development until chicks fledge. Overall, we are talking about a minimum of two months of daily visits, longer if the original nest is lost and the birds have to renest.

For plovers, creating a nest is always a gamble with poor odds of success. The likelihood of a nest remaining untouched for the twenty-five or so days needed for the eggs to hatch, and the chicks surviving another twenty-five to thirty days until fledging, is unpredictable. It is, to those of us who have watched the cycle over fifteen nesting seasons, a miracle that any chicks survive. But seeing a handful of chicks make it, season after season, brings a sense of reward. And seeing one fledge, take off for the first time, is exhilarating.

What might cause a nest to fail? Foxes, raccoons, skunks, and crows all find plover eggs to be a delicacy worth hunting for. Among these predators, the crow is arguably the most dangerous because of its high degree of intelligence. Sometimes, one finds crow tracks paralleling plover tracks for a hundred yards or more along the beach. Crows are smart enough to track plovers the way we do, and they no doubt find it easier than humans as they are much closer to the ground to begin with. They can also track humans tracking plovers. Some of us have come to view them as evil in spite of the fact that they are simply doing what crows do. Anyway, it seems more than coincidental that they only come in black.

High tides can spell disaster for a nest. Plovers try hard to locate their nests above the high tide line, marked by seaweed wrack. They have no way of anticipating when a twelve-foot tide (two feet higher than normal, sometimes called a "king tide") is coming. Nor do they know when a spring or summer storm will drive wave heights and push water high up the beach.

Scrapes are a precursor of nests. What is a scrape? Just that. The male excavates slight depressions in the sand, often in pebble-strewn areas, to impress the female. He may decorate the edge with small bits of broken shell. Sometimes she helps with this home decorating. A preponderance of scrapes in an area is a good indication that there will be a nest soon. Scrapes tell us where to erect protective fencing, also known as "symbolic fencing" because it will not actually keep determined people or wild animals out.

How do we find these scrapes, these small depressions in the sand easily confused with old footprints? Follow the plover tracks to them where possible. Rocky areas make this extremely difficult. If we are lucky, there will be several faint sets of prints leading back and forth to a scrape. Or we patiently watch for the birds to return to an area. And that is where we look for the first egg. Maintain a safe distance and watch through binoculars or a spotting scope.

When it comes to nest siting, these birds are very particular. For a plover nest to survive it is all about location: Above high tides. A place where eggs will blend in and become invisible among the pebbles that surround the nest. Away from the fox tracks that run along the dune grass edge. Away from trees on the bluff where crows roost to survey activity on the beach below. Away from people walking dogs. Near sparse vegetation to provide sun cover for young chicks. Given all these limitations, one can easily imagine that a large part of the beach landscape is ruled out by the birds as unsuitable for nesting.

Experience shows plovers make pretty good decisions. However, a beach like Ellisville's that may have been able to accommodate a greater number of nesting pairs ten years ago has been eroded by storms and reduced in area by the rising sea to the point that only two or three nesting pairs might be supportable today. As available space shrinks, plovers engage in territorial disputes throughout the spring and early summer. And long odds become very long odds when nests are placed in marginal locations. Tides take them, predators feast on the eggs, or, most painful to watch, crows grab unfledged chicks. Plover protectors go to great lengths to keep nests safe from predation, but some threats cannot be mitigated.

Keeping Nests Safe

There are strategies for dealing with certain predator threats, but they are controversial. One protective measure is something called an "exclosure." An exclosure is a ten-foot-diameter circle of wire fencing placed around a nest with eggs in it, relying on two-inch by four-inch openings to exclude anything larger than a plover. The circular structure is buried eight inches in the sand to foil tunneling access and covered tightly with fine nylon-mesh netting to keep crows out from above. Steel rebar posts are driven into the ground around the circle to anchor the fencing.

Erecting an exclosure is very much a team effort. It has to be, because the nest already contains eggs, and we cannot scare the birds away or cause an interruption to incubation lasting more than a few minutes. So a team of at least six people, led by someone licensed for exclosure work by the Commonwealth of Massachusetts, moves in from all sides at once and erects it. The goal is to be in and out within fifteen minutes. Risk factors such as time of day and weather must be considered.

Research shows that the odds of successful hatching rise significantly when an exclosure is deployed in a high-risk area. Unfortunately, there is a downside to this. Exclosures draw attention. From a distance, they look a bit like a round chicken coop. Crows may perch on top and cause the plovers to abandon the nest. People also take notice, and not all are sympathetic toward plovers. Some predators simply wait it out until chicks hatch and leave the exclosure, then grab them.

All of this begs questions. Should we interfere in timeless, natural conflicts and put the weight of our influence on the underdog's side? How much intervention is too much? Should a marksman be brought in to shoot crows? This is not a joke. Shooting crows is periodically suggested, and crows have been poisoned by wildlife authorities on Cape Cod. When does the level of protection extended to threatened species become interference with natural processes that have occurred for tens of thousands, if not millions, of years? Predation is a natural process that helps keep things in balance.

The Friends' team has learned over many nesting seasons that a light touch generally works best, focusing mainly on keeping humans at bay. Most people are not attuned to what is going on around them in a natural setting like Ellisville beach. As such, their behavior can be threatening to nests and unfledged chicks. But all of us share some blame. We are the ones who caused the near-extinction of the Piping Plover population to begin with.

A Cotton Ball on Two Toothpicks

Piping Plover nests typically contain three or four eggs. Finding a nest when it has just the first egg in it, a "one-egger," is ideal. The frequency with which we do that speaks to the level of skill and experience of our team. Indistinguishable from beach pebbles by design, the eggs are laid over a period of several days until the clutch is complete. Only then will the adult birds begin incubating the nest. Male and female take turns on the nest for the next three to four weeks. Incubation is for plovers a shared burden, and one often sees what amounts to a changing of the guard when one parent comes to relieve the other on the nest.

The birds are highly skilled at protecting their nests. When a predator or person approaches the vicinity of the nest, the bird on picket duty will draw attention to itself and run in a direction intended to lead the intruder away. For extremely close and imminent threats to the nest or unfledged chicks, the bird will feign a broken wing in hopes of presenting itself as easy prey. Sometimes it will drag two "broken" wings along the sand. Come even closer and the incubating bird will bolt from the nest and try the same gambit. Subterfuge is all they have. Most of the time, thankfully, it is enough.

Hatching of the eggs and the emergence of plover chicks is a heartwarming experience that members of the Friends' monitoring team have at times managed to witness. The chicks are tiny. And adorably fuzzy. The most apt description is "a cotton ball on two toothpicks." A sudden gust of wind sends them tumbling. Anyone seeing newly hatched chicks for the first time will not imagine that they will be trooping around the beach, foraging, and feeding themselves within a matter of hours. Piping Plover chicks are classified as precocial for this reason.

The chicks charge off in search of microscopic bugs that jump out of the rotting seaweed along the tide line, closely watched over by an accompanying parent. Even day-old chicks mimic the stop-and-go movement of their parents. If you take your eyes off them in the rocks, even momentarily, you may not find them again. In their early days they shelter under a parent whenever a warning cry goes up or to warm themselves. The visual effect of several chicks hiding under a parent's fluff is that of a many-legged plover. One memorable photo showing an adult plover with eight legs (hers plus those of her three chicks wedged underneath her) taken by Friends member Heidi Sanders was featured on the USFWS's Conserving the Nature of the Northeast website. The agency posted the image in commemoration of Mother's Day 2013.[3]

Members of the monitoring team visit the beach on a rotating schedule seven days a week from early April when the nesting season officially begins until late summer when the last chick has fledged or, in less successful years, when the possibilities for nests, eggs, and chicks have been exhausted. Once chicks are present, the nature of the visit necessarily changes from protection to monitoring. Team members count the chicks each day and enjoy watching their shenanigans.

There is often an independent-minded chick in the brood. He will explore far and wide, a good distance away from the watchful eye of one parent. At first, chicks have but stubs where the wings will develop. Yet within a matter of two weeks they grow to be almost equal in size to the adults, but with no neck rings in their first year and no orange on the bill, which remains all black. Without these clues, it would be hard to distinguish three-week-old chicks from adults.

Does maintaining the Ellisville Marsh inlet impact plover and tern nesting productivity? Yes, in a positive way. Although inlet maintenance mainly benefits the marsh system by keeping tidal flows going strong, there is also a key advantage for shorebirds nesting on the barrier beach, one that often escapes attention by regulators unfamiliar with the specific characteristics of the site.

It may be difficult to visualize, but when the inlet becomes partially blocked and the channel becomes elongated, its path cuts diagonally across the beach. The diverted channel effectively becomes a moat dividing the beach nesting area in half. Unfledged chicks are unable to cross the channel and are thus restricted to a smaller area where they are more vulnerable to being found by predators. Worse still, if chicks are caught on the barrier spit when the tide comes in, foxes, raccoons, and skunks can come down the narrow peninsula that serves as a land bridge from the state park, leaving the chicks no avenue for escape. People with dogs come down the land bridge onto the spit as well. Keeping the inlet open and the channel straight, narrow, and deep severs the land bridge and keeps people, dogs, and four-legged predators from entering the nesting area from the north, thereby improving unfledged chicks' odds of survival.

The year 2015 was typical for Piping Plovers at Ellisville Beach. Although there was only one nesting pair (Ellisville Beach has hosted as many as four pairs in other years), three chicks hatched and survived the twenty-five days necessary to fledge. It was touch and go for several weeks. High tides came within inches of overwashing the nest, predators took a Least Tern nest within fifty yards of the plover nest, and the beach was crowded with beachgoers during hot weekends throughout July. Thanks largely to the diligent efforts of their parent, nicknamed Muttonchops because his thick neck band resembled sideburns, three chicks fledged.

Traumatic Incidents and Other Challenges

The saddest part of Piping Plover monitoring comes when a nest has survived to full term and eggs have safely hatched, the chicks have been doing well and growing rapidly, and they are within days of their first tentative flight. A crow grabs a full-grown chick on the verge of flying. After having been present at virtually every stage of the nesting cycle, we have become bonded. We have given them names and recorded their growth stages and their antics in our daily logbook. You cannot help but grieve. The experience is like losing a beloved household pet. Mortality remains high among Piping Plovers.

Speaking of emotions, encounters with humans can be at times vexatious, at other times saddening. While most cooperate with guidelines to protect the birds and increase the chances that chicks will survive, some flout the rules and step over fencing. Others pretend ignorance, answering "Why, no" when asked, "Did you see that 'No Dogs Allowed on This Beach' sign you walked by when you arrived?" There is a widespread sense of entitlement that Friends volunteers struggle to understand. The property on Ellisville Beach where the plovers nest was never public, yet some claim rights based solely on the logic that "I've been doing this here for years."

Changing such ingrained behavior can be a challenge. Team members try to be diplomatic. "Could you please fly your kite farther down the beach? The birds that are nesting here think it's a predator," or "Please don't let your dog run loose over there. We have vulnerable, one-day-old chicks that can't fly." Some beachgoers behave aggressively. At least one member of the team has been physically threatened. Fencing is periodically vandalized. "No Dogs" signs erected by Erik Boyer, director of field operations for the Wildlands Trust, are torn up and tossed into patches of poison ivy. No matter. Team members go in and retrieve them.

Within a few days of erecting two small areas of fencing in March 2019 to protect Piping Plover nesting areas on Ellisville Beach within Shifting Lots Preserve, vandals had cut the twine in several places. As a condition of regulatory permits allowing maintenance of the salt marsh inlet, the Friends must erect "symbolic fencing" (fencing that is not capable of excluding wildlife but placed instead to signal beachgoers that nests are possible within the area) prior to April 1 of each year.

One miscreant returned several nights per week over a three-month period to slash the fencing lines. The motion-activated camera hidden in a cedar tree to catch the culprit captured some wonderful images of a coyote looking for food along the dune line, but no human vandal.

Threats to wildlife at Ellisville Marsh and Ellisville Beach do not stop there. Horseback riders have ignored signs prohibiting horses on the beach during shorebird nesting season posted by the Wildlands Trust at Shifting Lots Preserve. Hoofprints were found within a few feet of an area that was about to become a Piping Plover nest (as indicated by scrapes). All-terrain vehicles and fat-tired bicycles on the beach pose additional threats.

Having local residents monitor the nesting area on a daily basis means less fencing needs to be put up. Because the volunteer monitoring team knows where past nests have been found, they are able to make an educated guess as to where they might nest in the upcoming season and thus minimize the area of the beach that's off-limits. This benefit is generally overlooked or taken for granted by people in the neighborhood. But there is a more direct effect: people who know that their neighbors are the ones protecting the nests and chicks are more likely to cooperate. Who wants to run into a neighbor on the street or at a neighborhood get-together after a testy exchange over birds on the beach? We are inevitably more temperate in our dealings with people we will see again.

One key to changing behavior is to influence adults through their children. When a young child is shown a plover chick through a set of binoculars for the first time and understands that they have been hiding in plain sight nearby all afternoon, the impact is immediate and palpable. When a child marvels at such a discovery, it is hard for parents not to soften their views. Thank goodness for children.

Those who patrol the beach on a daily basis throughout the

summer receive their own rewards. These birds have unique appearances and personalities one can relate to. Muttonchops waited patiently for a mate to show up for nearly three weeks one year. Fat Boy was a huge chick whose voracious appetite delayed his inaugural flight by almost a week. In the end, he had to be chased into the air. Waldo, a female so-named by ecologist and then-PhD candidate Michelle Stantial because she was so hard to locate, was banded as a chick on a beach in Sandwich, Massachusetts, in 2012. Waldo nested on Ellisville Beach for two years and later returned to her roots in Sandwich.

The Ups and Downs of Plover Protection

Part of the fun of being a nest monitor is trying to imagine what the birds are thinking. Some of them seem to glare at nest monitors. Others are so trusting they allow team members to get close to their unfledged chicks. Not so with other plovers intent on getting too close when there are eggs or chicks present. Some years there is what Paula Marcoux calls a "crazy aunt," a plover that repeatedly approaches the nest or chicks of another pair, thus sowing chaos and discord.

The team witnesses a variety of other plover conflicts as well, over contested territory and desirable mates. One has to laugh at plover fights. No one is ever hurt. One plover fluffs its feathers up, inflating itself to become as large as possible, and then charges at the other. There never seems to be actual contact.

Fights with crows are another thing entirely. Piping Plovers are fearless. Volunteers have seen them chasing crows several times their size in the sky. We humans have chased the crows, too, throwing rocks and, once or twice, banging on metal pans with sticks to discourage them. Ellisville crows seem to take notice of the Friends' volunteers—they sense hostility and take off as we approach.

Team members afford themselves a degree of artistic license in their online daily monitoring reports. One May 2020 entry read as follows: "Nest 1A now has four eggs and is being incubated. Nobody home when I approached. Did my rounds and five minutes later found her back on nest. Another pair active twenty yards east of scraggly tree. He wanted to mate and did his best storm-trooper step but she wanted no part of it. He left sulking and dejected. This female is the one with the light-brown neck band that doesn't go all the way round her front. Very pretty girl."

Volunteers can go to great lengths to protect unfledged chicks. In one instance, Waldo produced four chicks whose safety was immediately threatened by the presence of crows. Friends members mounted a protective vigil, starting as early as 6:00 a.m. and covering many of the morning hours when crows are most likely to strike. Led by stalwart Rosemary Smith, volunteers shadowed the chicks and their parental chaperone up and down the beach, maintaining a safe distance and keeping the crows at bay. Other volunteers joined the cause.

All four chicks survived the next ten days, gaining weight and learning how to blend in perfectly with the beach. But in a sad turn, three of the four chicks were taken by predators shortly thereafter. Only one chick remained. She flew a few weeks later, salvaging the summer's work in what can only be described as a small miracle. Her given name? Little Rosemary. Turns out it takes a village to raise a plover chick.

In another instance, which fell well outside accepted plover monitoring practice, several team members rendezvoused on the beach just before midnight one evening when it seemed inevitable that a nest would be overwashed by the tide at full moon. Volunteers are always careful not to get too close to a nest during incubation as this puts the eggs at risk. But here were three grown adults, lying flat on their backs in the dark, pushing sandpiles toward a nest with their feet while a plover sat on it quietly, peering curiously at the humans' odd behavior.

The tide was thwarted by the low sand berm that was improvised that night, the bird remained on the nest, and the memory has never faded from the minds of those who turned out. Perhaps she understood what her protectors were trying to do. If so, she probably thought, "Crazy humans . . . what will they do next?"

The Allies Have Landed

The Least Tern is another threatened shorebird species that nests at Ellisville Beach. Least terns made only a few attempts to establish a nesting colony in the early years of the Friends' shorebird-monitoring program. But as the inlet was stabilized, the terrain south of the inlet became rockier and cobble ridges formed over time. The birds found this beach landscape more to their liking. As many as fifteen to twenty Least Tern nests are now seen in years when they come.

The year 2019 seemed to be when Least Terns began to take notice of Ellisville Beach as a nesting site—dozens began to show up. For the first time in years, a nesting colony formed. Then, as the number of birds grew, the colony doubled in size, expanding to a new area on the outer barrier spit. As many as thirty birds eventually took up residence, creating between ten and fifteen nests. Both Piping Plovers and Least Terns appeared to favor the camouflage afforded by the cobble near the inlet. It helped that predators do not frequent this area as much, keeping mainly to the dune grass edge. Although it is always difficult to get an accurate count of Least Tern chicks because the adult birds fiercely protect their colony, 2019 marked the start of several successful seasons.

Least Terns behave differently from Piping Plovers. The nests can be quite close to one another in a colony, whereas Piping Plovers are territorial and spar over space. There are fewer eggs in Least Tern nests, usually two or three. Their chicks are not precocial: parents feed them small fish for weeks and continue to feed them even after they fledge. And the adult birds do not simply rely on camouflage or the pretense of a broken wing for protection of their nests and chicks but instead dive-bomb uninvited guests. Diane Jordan has learned the hard way that a price is paid when one gets close enough to a Least Tern nest or chick for a sharp photo. She comes away covered in bird droppings the adult birds have rained down on her during their strafing runs.

There is a significant advantage to the Piping Plovers that accrues from Least Terns nesting in close proximity to them on Ellisville Beach. The presence of a colony helps protect plover nests. Humans and dogs seem to get the message fairly quickly when a line of Least Terns homes in on them and flies over within a few feet of their heads squawking loudly. Whether the plovers actually appreciate the air defense provided by their distant bird cousin is unclear.

An Especially Memorable Season

Each year of nest monitoring brings moments of joy, disappointment, and a flood of other emotions. After fourteen years, team members may have thought they had seen all the possible variations on the theme and experienced all the emotions. But 2020 exploded that myth and raised the level of drama to a new height. Instead of a single nesting pair, the norm in recent nesting seasons, three pairs of Piping Plovers showed up in May. Their territorial aggression became manifest immediately as squabbles were seen up and down the narrow beach. It was remarkable that any were able to nest. But nest they did.

The nests appeared in quick succession, each holding four eggs. One was washed over by a high tide driven higher by the full moon. The other two were incubated for weeks, and four chicks hatched on schedule in one of them. The last nest became an object of fascination.

Something seemed off about the third nest. The parents would come and go rather than incubate the eggs continuously. Such unusual behavior augurs badly for the success of the nest. Then team members noticed through binoculars that several eggs were uncovered and exposed to the elements while the nest was being incubated. A bad sign indeed. The female of the pair was small in size and unable to fully cover the nest. The real problem, it turned out, was that there were seven eggs in the nest, a rarity for this species. The most likely explanation is that two females laid eggs in the same nest, sometimes called "egg-dumping." This theory was reinforced when a second female repeatedly attempted to reach the nest and was chased off by the incubating bird or its partner.

Two chicks ultimately hatched about ten days late but were underdeveloped and did not survive. The other eggs eventually began to rot in the nest. The smell must have attracted foxes, which not only ate the rotten eggs but wiped out the renest of another pair and most of the Least Tern colony in the bargain.

What would be remembered most from the summer of 2020 tragedy? The touching fact that the adult birds continued to incubate the ill-fated nest for forty-eight days straight, double the normal incubation period. They do not give up easily, even when the odds are very long.

The drama ended with some happy news though. All four chicks from the first nest survived long enough to fledge. The team had been unable to locate one of the chicks for several weeks and had reluctantly concluded that it had been lost, but this one was apparently independent-minded and felt no need to hang out with the three siblings. Three gangly Least Tern chicks also fattened up and fledged.

Seeing a nesting cycle through to successful completion and watching chicks fly only adds to the enduring connection team members have with Piping Plovers and Least Terns on Ellisville Beach. The experience helps sustain us through long New England winters.

One can never fully understand how the chicks instinctively know what to do next. The female parent often departs after the chicks hatch. The male parent takes off once the surviving chicks have fledged. The chicks themselves spend the month after their first flight feeding and building flying experience, swooping low over the beach and hanging out together. Then they, too, fly off, covering a thousand miles in a trip to a distant place they have never been via a route they have never traveled. It boggles the mind.

These birds are, against the greatest of odds, survivors. Friends' team members have learned a great deal about life from them. What is the single, most important lesson we have gained from working with Piping Plovers? It is that their fight is also our fight.

However, threats to shorebirds are only part of the story here. Existential threats also exist to water resources and to those who rely on them—plants, wildlife, and, of course, people. Protecting nature against harm cannot be limited to threatened birds or even the salt marsh ecosystem. It must encompass the estuary and the larger Ellisville watershed.

CHAPTER 10
Detoxifying a Pond

FOLLOWING A HERRING BROOK upstream from Ellisville Marsh, one comes to lovely, spring-fed pond. Savery Pond forms the headwaters of a creek known locally as the "Herring Brook," one of two freshwater inputs to the Ellisville estuary. With its tree-lined shores and few neighbors, Savery seems isolated, sparkling, and pristine—unless you have visited in the heat of summer in the last few years, that is. The Massachusetts Department of Public Health has periodically closed the pond because of dangerous levels of toxic blue-green algae, also known as cyanobacteria.

The "Herring Brook" runs to the western edge of Ellisville Marsh. The water leaves the pond where a wooden board in a concrete slot used to serve as a flow gate. Further along, the stream enters the marsh just beyond another old flow gate near a slicked-down path in the grass on the bank made by otters. Nowadays the water trickles around the rocks in the streambed. River herring no longer run here.

A crushed culvert several hundred yards up the brook in the woods makes fish passage nearly impossible. If the fish were able to reach their former spawning grounds at Savery Pond, they might find it to be an inhospitable place, periodically beset with blue-green algae. When the algae appear, the pond is dangerous: No swimming. Do not eat the fish. Do not let your dog drink the water. Cyanobacteria produce a potent neurotoxin, thus it may be good that the hydraulic connection between the pond and Ellisville Marsh is broken. The brook runs parallel to a centuries-old dirt road.

Old Sandwich Road wends its way from Ellisville Marsh five miles through scrub pine and oak forest to Chiltonville, one of Plymouth's oldest villages. For almost its entire length the road is dirt and gravel, as it was when it served travelers on horseback and in carriages between Plymouth and Sandwich. It is best to be on the road in winter when the hard-packed, rutted surface is frozen. Spring rains turn it muddy, and in the summer winds and wheels whip up dust that can paint a car gritty brown in no time. Near the road's southern end, behind a vintage colonial with fieldstone walls, one can see the sunlight glinting off the pond.

The pond itself covers twenty-nine acres and is classified as a Massachusetts "great pond."[1] It is hemmed in by a disparate set of land uses—a residential subdivision, mixed deciduous and evergreen forest, and a commercial recreational vehicle park.

Eleven acres of cranberry bogs operated next to the pond for more than seventy years. One bog was recently purchased and converted to conservation land by the town. Another has been taken out of commercial operation. The fact that neither bog is actively farmed is good news for the pond. Fertilizers and chemical treatments are not being added, which reduces the level of nutrient runoff into the pond. In between the old bogs, Savery Pond plays a key role in the ecology of the Ellisville watershed and in its own modest way influences the health of the Ellisville estuary and salt marsh.

Savery Pond was not on the radar screen when the effort to revitalize Ellisville Marsh began in 2007. The pond's freshwater input to the marsh is hardly noticeable. The stream flow is a rounding error in the marsh's hydraulic equation—a few thousand gallons of freshwater pitted against the fifty million gallons or more of saltwater that makes its way through the inlet during each six-hour tide cycle.

These two water resources—the Ellisville estuary and Savery Pond—are the joint centerpieces of the Ellisville watershed, the ecological system that gives life to plants and wildlife within this natural domain. The two have a synergistic relationship. Freshwater from the pond makes its way to the Ellisville estuary. Fish swim upstream to take advantage of the riverine and pond habitats. At least they did in the past.

The herring run is a fragile connection. It winds its way narrowly through the woods along Old Sandwich Road, unseen except by those who walk the old path there. The path runs from the base of the dirt road to the cranberry bog. It is a favorite place of night people—a trash-strewn pull-off, well out of view from the road, a remote place for meeting up. Old burnt offerings line a fire pit. There's a charred mattress. Rusty bed springs. Smashed bottles. Soggy cigarette butts.

Getting there is what caused harm to the herring run. The wheels of pickup trucks collapsed the small culvert under the path and greatly slowed the flow of water going downstream toward its marsh escape. A swampy backup, plants mired in the stagnant water, has formed on the upstream side. Only a small and very determined fish could pass safely through to reach the pond a quarter mile upstream.

The possibility that the stream could be restored so that herring might return to spawn in Savery Pond would not have occurred to anyone associated with the Ellisville Marsh project had it not been for other herring runs that have recently been restored by the Town of Plymouth. But the restoration of this particular herring run is a chapter yet to be written.

It became apparent to the Friends that Savery Pond needed help. Savery Pond was reported to have the highest nutrient (nitrogen/ phosphorous) concentrations of thirty-eight Plymouth ponds listed in the Town's 2015 *Pond and Lake Atlas.*[2] Total phosphorous concentration was literally "off the chart" compared with other ponds included in the report. Although blue-green algal blooms had been seen in the pond for many years, they had become almost an annual event, occurring in 2011 and 2014–17.

This ominous pattern of toxic, algal blooms meant that Savery Pond was considered the Plymouth pond with the most degraded water quality.[3] This was quite a distinction considering the sheer number of ponds in town.

Pond Monitoring Begins

From its founding in 2007 until 2012, the Friends focused all of its attention on restoring the Ellisville salt marsh. The Ellisville estuary, the freshwater side of the system, received less attention. However, the Friends' board in 2012 began to discuss broadening the nonprofit's mission to cover the wider Ellisville watershed. Armed with a grant from the New England Grassroots Environmental Fund,[4] the Friends were able to undertake a baseline water quality monitoring project at Savery Pond that summer.

There had been a serious outbreak of blue-green algae the previous summer, which necessitated the closing of the pond to swimming, fishing, and everything else. Left unaddressed, this recurring problem could ultimately have a harmful effect on wildlife and fisheries in Ellisville Marsh downstream.

It helped that Paula Marcoux lived on the pond and, along with Ellen Russell, had assisted in past water quality sampling there as part of the Massachusetts Estuaries Project conducted by the University of Massachusetts (UMass)–Dartmouth. However, after the Friends' grant study of baseline water quality was completed, no further action was immediately forthcoming to address the chronic issues.

The focus on Savery Pond's water quality brought to the Friends' attention an individual who was both capable of understanding the technical issues and highly motivated to find a solution: Peter Schwartzman. Schwartzman worked alongside Marcoux on the Friends' 2012 baseline study, which became the cornerstone of what came to be known as the Friends' Savery Pond Initiative. His family has owned a cottage on Savery Pond

since the early 1940s, so he also had a vested interest in addressing the pond's environmental problems, just as Lookout Point
homeowners had a vested interest in solving the bluff erosion
problem when the Friends were first formed.

A Driving Force

Meeting Schwartzman for the first time gives one the impression
that he is an individual who can get things done. He is tall and
speaks softly but earnestly. No-nonsense manner. Speaks his
mind. Holds nothing back. Explains everything patiently and in
great detail. Leaves no stone unturned. Better yet: he is a licensed
hydrogeologist.

Within six months of his initial involvement, Schwartzman
was elected to the Friends' board. He became the rallying point
for a continuing series of projects and actions over the next several years that moved the Friends closer to a scientific explanation
for the repeated cyanobacteria outbreaks at Savery Pond.

To say that Schwartzman is driven would be an understate-
ment. Relentless is a better descriptor. The volume of emails
coming from him totaled those from the other nine board members combined, twice over. To work with Schwartzman is like
asking for a drink of water and having a fire hose turned on you.
To be fair though, he operated at a more granular level than
the rest of the Friends' board and surfaced issues that others
could not have. Without him, the Friends' Savery Pond Initiative
would not have progressed at the pace it did, if at all. To understand the causes of the problem and weigh possible remedies, the
Friends began working with the Cape Cod Cranberry Growers
Association, UMass Cranberry Station, the Town of Plymouth,
the School for Marine Science and Technology (SMAST) at
UMass–Dartmouth, the US Department of Agriculture, and a
neighboring cranberry bog operator.

The Town Weighs In

The Friends' Savery Pond Initiative established a working relationship with David Gould's Department of Marine and Environmental Affairs at an opportune time. Other ponds in Plymouth were being impacted by cyanobacteria. Kim Tower, an environmental technician in the department, made a point of staying close to the work at Savery Pond, viewing the Friends' project as a possible model for community action that could be replicated elsewhere in town. For a time, she also served on the Friends' board.

Tower spearheaded much of the Town's work with guidance from SMAST. The Friends provided assistance. The relationship between the Town and the Friends quickly became a public-private partnership, albeit on a small scale. Tower organized and carried out data collection, provided technical assistance, arranged for the town to underwrite the cost of laboratory testing of water samples, ran interference with outside consultants, and advocated for the town to support the project. She and her boss, David Gould, it must be said, exemplify the kind of public employees the Friends had naively hoped would champion the cause of revitalizing Ellisville Marsh. Perhaps they would champion pond restoration now. Would that the other agencies the Friends dealt with had people like these two.

For his part, Schwartzman had been trying to get the bog owner adjacent to Savery Pond to allow the Friends to collect nutrient data on his bog for several years—communicating by email or through his tenant farmer, but not directly. As Schwartzman recalls, "I was persistent, and finally he agreed to meet me for coffee at a local haunt, 'The Blueberry Muffin.' With me I brought a jar of thick, green, soupy water taken from the pond that morning. I showed it to him and said, 'This is the pond!' To which he responded that he'd been thinking of selling the bog, as it wasn't really a moneymaker. Apparently, he had never seen all the letters from the Plymouth Conservation Commission expressing interest in purchasing the bog. It took an in-person meeting and putting the pond water in front of his face to see!"[5]

In late 2016, Plymouth Town Meeting voted to use Community Preservation Act (CPA) funds for the $250,000 purchase of the 11.5-acre property adjacent to Savery Pond, the key feature of which was the 6.5-acre cranberry bog. The removal from commercial operation of the cranberry bog was expected to contribute to improved water quality in Savery Pond and the surrounding watershed, protecting several town wells in the bargain. Friends' board members Schwartzman and Marcoux worked tirelessly to make the initial connection between the bog owner and town staff, attended meetings, and worked with local residents and Town Meeting members to garner the support necessary for passage of the measure. They pitched the project with enthusiasm and, more important, facts about the bog's impact on Savery Pond.

The town's purchase of the bog was not the end of the story though. Monitoring data suggest that, along with ongoing nutrient inputs (from agriculture, landscaping, stormwater, septic discharge to groundwater), the sediments on the bottom of the pond experience low oxygen ("anoxic") conditions that may liberate accumulated "legacy" nutrients and contribute to ongoing algae blooms.

The Town's 2016 decision to acquire the commercially active cranberry bog adjacent to the pond and return it to its previous, natural grassland state was a turning point. There has not been a blue-green algal bloom at Savery Pond since 2017, although other factors might help explain this. And from the Town's standpoint, the Savery Pond Initiative represented a citizen-based model for addressing water quality problems at other distressed Plymouth ponds.

Algae other than cyanobacteria are nevertheless still present in the pond, according to Schwartzman: "Fifty years ago, the water was so clear my grandmother would throw quarters into the sandy sediment, and we would see them and dive for them. Now, you can hardly keep your eyes open in the water without feeling the sting of algae and would be lucky to be able to see the bottom to track a coin! So we are still 'impacted,' and it's not 'back to normal'—just improved. We will have to see what happens in the future."[6]

More Distressed Ponds

Savery Pond is by no means the only Plymouth water resource to have been impacted by toxic blue-green algae. Bartlett Pond is a thirty-three-acre pond several miles north of Ellisville that flows into Cape Cod Bay at White Horse Beach, a wide expanse of flat sand packed with beachgoers on hot summer days. This pond, too, has suffered cyanobacteria outbreaks over the years.

In the case of Bartlett Pond, however, the cyanobacteria are made up by a different species (*Chroococcus*), which makes it invisible. There is no pea-soup appearance. The bacteria are only detectable by periodic water testing. Too much nitrogen spurs these algae to form. Where does the nitrogen come from? Most likely, runoff or leaching from nearby septic systems and applications of lawn fertilizers.

The consequences of a 2018 algal bloom at Bartlett were even more disturbing than those that had been seen at Savery Pond: "Rotting fish float just beneath the surface, suffocated by a lack of oxygen, which was used up by the algae. On the bottom of the pond, freshwater mussels suffered the same fate, and floated to the surface. While nearby White Horse Beach, which receives outflow from the pond, isn't closed, residents are still being cautioned. As of July 17 Bartlett Pond has been closed, likely for the rest of the summer."[7]

If the Savery Pond experience illustrates the value of a proactive, neighborhood-based effort to get water quality problems under control, Bartlett shows what happens in its absence. One can imagine the same problem occurring many more times at other Plymouth ponds. Indeed, 2020 saw cyanobacteria blooms at Great Herring Pond, Plymouth's largest at 376 acres, and two others as scant winter snow, higher summer temperatures, and particularly dry summer months tilted an already fragile balance toward crisis. Climate change plays a role here.

A New Nonprofit is Formed

The project the Friends initiated in 2012 with the baseline water quality assessment at Savery Pond had matured and reached critical mass by 2019, spinning off from the Friends as its own independent 501(c)(3) nonprofit. It became the Savery Pond Conservancy.[8] The new nonprofit is focused exclusively on the health of Savery Pond, building on past accomplishments of the Friends' Savery Pond Initiative.

Under Schwartzman's leadership, the project took another leap forward later that year as Plymouth Town Meeting approved funding for development of a Watershed Study and Management Plan for Savery Pond. The Town of Plymouth and the conservancy began jointly funding the sampling of lake sediments to determine the role of accumulated legacy nutrients in fueling algal blooms. Paula Marcoux joined the new board, making it her third seat on local nonprofit boards. So did Roger Janson, the former sea mosser.

This coming of age of an environmental project closely aligned with the revitalization of Ellisville Marsh reinforces an essential element of the Friends' experience. When you pass through one doorway, another opens. You cannot predict where the journey will lead. Just listen to your heart and welcome others to join you. Nature will show you the way. Nature is full of small pleasures that delight us and inspire us to act. Simply being present in a special place is often enough.

CHAPTER 11

Natural Wonders

THE PLEASURES SERVED UP by nature occur on a schedule that cannot be predicted. They just happen. One is in the right place at the right time. It is that simple.

In August 2020, a 260-foot steel super yacht named the *Felix* anchored a mile offshore from Ellisville for the night. Through a spotting scope, my wife, Christine, and I could see people being served a meal alfresco on the upper deck by crew members in dark-colored shirts. The next day we sailed our twelve-foot, bright-yellow sailboat out to see the *Felix* up close—the yacht was impressive.

A few years earlier, on an unseasonably warm Columbus Day, we had sailed our boat to roughly the same position when a splash nearby caught our attention. Turning through the wind to investigate we found ourselves surrounded by a pod of dolphins. They seemed to revel at playing with our tiny boat, swimming excitedly alongside, arcing ahead of us, gliding upside down under the boat so closely that one rubbed against the hull and popped the rudder. Pure joy all around. In that moment we became children again. Give me dolphins over a yacht any day.

Birds That Delight

The pleasure of kayaking into the marsh around the high tide is one of Christine's favorite summertime escapes. She floats in on the rising tide, needing only to steer here and there to avoid scraping against rocks in the shallows along the channel edge. After a half hour or so of exploration, she glides effortlessly back out on the ebbing tide. I cannot recall what led me to first try this or when it was. I got in my kayak and off I went.

As I floated by the large sandbar that had accreted in the old harbor, I spotted an unusual-looking shorebird. It was quite impressive, perhaps eighteen inches tall, with what looked like an orange sock pulled over its head and neck. It had pronounced black-and-white stripes on its folded wings and was not at all shy. All the gulls and yellowlegs had flown off as I approached. Most notable of all, its elegant, four-inch-long bill was curved upward like some sort of scimitar.

I am not an experienced birder. I only expand my repertoire when I come across unfamiliar birds. And this was an unfamiliar species. Back at the house, it was not difficult to identify the bird. It was on the cover of Mass Audubon's calendar that year—an American Avocet. An email to Becky Harris returned information that this was no ordinary visitor to Massachusetts: a rare sighting at any time of the year; it usually remains well south.

Wayne Petersen, who has led Mass Audubon's Important Bird Area (IBA) program for many years, got wind and reported it—the first sighting of an American Avocet in the state that year. Two days later, a similar sighting came in from the North Shore. Same wayward bird perhaps? I have seen avocets on Florida beaches since that day. Each time serves to remind me that Ellisville Marsh is a place endowed with limitless natural possibilities.

What do an American Avocet, a Sandhill Crane, and a Harlequin Duck have in common? They are uncommon in southeastern Massachusetts. Yet all three have been seen in Ellisville Marsh or near the adjacent barrier beach in recent years, along with other rarely sighted species. Brilliantly patterned Harlequin Ducks are not typically found around Ellisville, yet they miraculously appear at the Ellisville inlet after a hurricane or nor'easter has struck and the surf is still churning angrily. They seem to love the tumult, the rough, up-and-down roller-coaster ride among white-capped breakers. One spent three days in the rough surf at the mouth of the Ellisville inlet after Tropical Storm Jose passed through in September 2017. These birds are a treat to see with their striking paintbrush strokes of gray, white, and black. They are a gift storms leave in their wake.

Years earlier there had been another, much different birding delight. From the top of the bluff in front of our house we could see a crowd of large white birds diving straight down from what seemed like a great height and entering the water of the bay with hardly a ripple. Every element of their body from head to tail feathers seemed sleek and streamlined. Their wings folded in so perfectly they all but disappeared into the water. No splash whatsoever as they knifed into the sea. Even more impressive, many dove simultaneously, unconcerned that they were puncturing the same small surface of water all at once, seemingly inches apart.

These birds with their black wingtips and light brown crowns, it turned out, were Northern Gannets, birds that remain at sea for most of their lives and are for this reason classified as pelagic. They use their webbed feet to propel themselves to great depths—seventy feet by some accounts—in search of fish. I had never seen one before, and here were fifty or more on our doorstep. I could have watched their display for hours. But this was a one-time extravaganza. Nature is full of evanescent delights.

Elusive Turtles

Mid-January on a New England shore can be a frigid time. It certainly was in 2016 when a local couple, Leah and Brad Bares, were walking their two-year-old Newfoundland dog, Veda, on Ellisville Beach. Newfoundlands are a breed known for rescuing fishermen, so it may not have been surprising when Veda found something unusual and lay down at the shoreline to get her owners' attention. Under a mound of seaweed was a forty-pound loggerhead turtle that had become cold-shocked and was at imminent risk of death from hypothermia. Winter strandings of sea turtles in the southern part of Cape Cod Bay are common as southbound migrating turtles find themselves blocked by the long elbow of the Cape.

The sea turtle was rescued and taken to the New England Aquarium for warming and rehabilitation. "Newfie," as the turtle was named in honor of its 120-pound rescuer, was released back into the ocean at Assateague, Maryland, that June with eight other rescued sea turtles. According to the New England Aquarium, Newfie's mid-January rescue was at the time the latest recorded date for a sea turtle to survive a winter stranding.[1]

The Bares's experience reinforces the theme that our relationship with nature can often be expressed in one-to-one terms. Each of us can find opportunities to relate to individuals in the natural system we are part of, whether it be Piping Plovers we have come to know over several nesting seasons or a sea turtle in dire need of help in the dead of winter.

Newfie was not the only turtle to come ashore in Ellisville. Others come to lay eggs in the dunes. These are likely to include Northern Diamondback Terrapins. Every year or two for the past decade, in June or July, sometimes as early as May, beachgoers have found an odd pattern of tracks leaving the bay and heading toward the dunes. Sometimes the tracks begin at the water's edge, lead toward the base of the coastal bank, and exhibit a U-turn back to the water when no dune is encountered. The tracks resemble a motorcycle tread bordered on either side by a series of dots. The tread mark is made by the turtle's shell, dragged along by the clawed feet on either side, which creates the dot pattern.

It must be a struggle to carry a heavy shell up the beach on your back over loose sand. None of us has actually seen these turtles, but the tracks are unmistakable. Where are they going, and why? They are most likely females coming ashore to lay their eggs above the high tide line. Once the eggs hatch, after some seventy days, the hatchlings make their way into the marsh and spend up to four years in the upper, grassy areas of the marsh where the salt meadow cordgrass grows.

The species thrives in brackish conditions, so the back part of Ellisville Marsh offers the perfect environment. And the terrapins need a safe place. They are classified as a threatened species in Massachusetts. Why are there so few? Because of us, just as with Piping Plovers. Humans feasted on the turtles as a delicacy throughout the nineteenth century. There is something as troubling about eating a turtle species into near extinction as there is in wearing Piping Plover–feathered hats. Threats to this species remain: there is still a market for the meat in Asia, an illegal pet trade, a lack of suitable nesting habitat, and high mortality at road crossings.

Turtle wonders in Ellisville are not limited to the shorefront. As discussed above, an old bog exists that is now a pond adjacent to Ellisville Marsh. Its ownership is shared by several property owners, two of whom occupy the oldest homes in the area, facing off across the pond on small hillocks, like sentinels. One of these old houses was lived in by Al Marsh and his family for years. Red-winged Blackbirds play in the cattails that line the banks of the pond, bouncing up and down on the thin stalks. The males revel in their colorful attractiveness to the opposite sex. They resemble soldiers in formal dress uniform with red and yellow epaulets on their shoulders.

One day as Christine and I made our way down the long gravel driveway to the pond to watch the blackbirds, we caught a glimpse of what appeared to be a beaver lolling in a small cove of the pond. But there are no beavers here. We made a quick return to the house to retrieve binoculars. It was a common snapping turtle. A large snapping turtle. A *mythically* large turtle. Its head appeared larger than a man's fist, and it rolled around slowly in the water, its shell glinting sunlight between patches of what looked like moss. At first we thought it must be a pair of turtles, perhaps in a mating embrace. But no, it was a solitary turtle. Its carapace, the length from the top to the bottom of its shell, looked to be thirty inches or more based on visual comparisons with the height of nearby reeds. We could not get closer for a better look due to the swampy terrain.

Subsequent research indicated that the largest snapping turtle ever captured in the United States had a carapace of nineteen and a half inches, with the exception of a large subspecies found in the Everglades called the alligator snapping turtle. Surely ours was larger. Outreach to the Massachusetts State herpetologist (at least five states besides Massachusetts have such a position) confirmed the largest size on record. The expert expressed skepticism about our observation and suggested our eyes might have been deceiving us.

A call to Ellen Russell, one of the property owners, yielded photos of a large female snapping turtle nesting in a dirt mound in 1991, twenty years earlier. Russell's snapper appeared to rival the US record holder in size. Could this be the same female two decades later? The state's expert predicted we might never see this turtle again. So far he has been right. Perhaps twenty years hence someone will be walking along the bank of the pond admiring the blackbirds will happen upon her. Fortunately, she has no natural predators in her habitat, nor are there any motorized boats. Snapping turtles can live one hundred years. This one may already be older than we are.

Whales and Seals

Round boulders punctuate the waters around Ellisville at low tide. One in particular resembles a whale and has long been nicknamed "Whale Rock" by locals. It is one of the largest boulders close to shore and a navigational hazard to boats. It lurks only a couple of feet below the surface even at high tide. It is actually a pair of rocks: the larger one forms the whale's head, and the smaller one the tail. Whale Rock is one of the first boulders to reappear as the tide goes out. It is often out there by itself, the most sought-after resting place for harbor seals on sun-drenched days.

During morning coffee on our porch in early May, Christine noticed that several new boulders had emerged offshore, beyond Whale Rock. Judy Quinn had also seen them and begun calling around. Diane Jordan, too, had noticed, out at dawn taking sunrise photographs from the top of the bluff. Binoculars made for instant identification. It was a group of endangered North Atlantic right whales that had gathered at the southern end of Cape Cod Bay to feed, their boulder-like heads appearing to be encrusted with barnacles. According to the National Oceanic and Atmospheric Administration (NOAA), "Their heads have knobby white patches of rough skin, called callosities, which appear white because of whale lice (cyamids) covering their otherwise black skin. Each right whale has a unique pattern of callosities that scientists use to identify individual whales, an invaluable tool in tracking population size and health. Aerial and ship-based surveys and the North Atlantic Right Whale Consortium's photo-identification database maintained by our partners at the New England Aquarium help track individuals over the years."[2]

It is a rare treat to have sixteen or more of these giants gathered in plain view just off our shores. The pod represented a small but significant percentage of the total estimated population of 350 left in the Atlantic. The adults weigh as much as seventy tons and run up to fifty-two feet in length. By noon a NOAA spotter plane was circling overhead, and shipping in the area had been ordered to stay below ten knots. They were safe, for the time being. A mother and calf later ventured close to the Ellisville inlet.

Another delight of summer in Ellisville is the sound of the Baker grandkids—John and his younger twin brothers, Peter and Michael—whooping it up on the beach. They come from landlocked Pennsylvania every summer with their parents, Steve and Erin, to spend a week or two at the family's rustic cottage on Lookout Point. Theirs is a multigenerational family tradition.

Whenever the Baker family comes, I am reminded that my parents brought me and my brother and sister from suburban New Jersey to a rental cottage on the shores of Cape Cod Bay in the 1950s. Perhaps when the Baker kids are seventy, they will remember as vividly as I do what it felt like to spend summer days at a small cottage on Cape Cod Bay surrounded by natural wonders so many years earlier. For suburban New Jersey kids like me and my siblings, it was a trip to the moon.

Most days the Baker kids are on the beach, and their escapades and experiences are unremarkable. The air is often pierced by their happy cries. They play on the rock groin near the cottage. Dig pits in the sandbars at low tide. Ride around in the not-fully-inflated inflatable that Steve picked up secondhand somewhere. Float in the cold-water shallows with life jackets or tubes. This is what they do when they are here, every day, even on days when it is raining lightly.

Like migrating birds, the Baker kids become an integral part of the Ellisville ecosystem for a time, released into the wild by their parents. They delight by simply being here. They absorb energy from the place and store it for their trip through the months that follow. And sometimes they get lucky—they are here at precisely the right moment to witness a spectacle. On one occasion, they were startled and thrilled to see a good-sized humpback whale feeding just a few hundred yards offshore in water perhaps only fifty feet deep. The whale remained for a few hours, disappearing as quietly as she had appeared. We saw her spouting from our little sailboat later that day but kept our distance. A twelve-foot fiberglass sailboat is no match for a fifty-foot whale. Dolphins are much safer to be around.

A small sailboat is the perfect platform from which to observe the goings-on in a rich, natural environment like Ellisville: Moves soundlessly. Harmless to marine life. Mostly random in its progress. Goes where the wind tells it to. We often see the frogman-like heads of seals, harbor or gray, popping up in our wake, curious to see what just went by. Some swim toward the boat to get a closer look.

Sailing through an area off the state park beach where the seals gather in large numbers can be a little unsettling. Dark, shiny heads appear on either side of the boat, almost daring you to pass through. Is this an attempt to intimidate trespassers? One begins to suspect so when one jumps out of the water and lands behind the boat with a loud slap. Perhaps they have a sense of humor and like to play tricks. One can hear what sounds like laughter coming from their rock perches at low tide some mornings. Do seals share jokes?

Natural wonders come in many forms and sizes, from the humpback whale feeding near shore to the tiny butterfly that alights on your sailboat a mile out in the ocean. To appreciate the astonishing biodiversity in a place like Ellisville, you need only attune your senses to your surroundings—stop, look, listen, feel the breeze, catch an aroma. Let your daily encounters fill you with wonder. Let yourself become a child again. Do it now, for you may not have the chance again.

CHAPTER 12

Canary in the Coal Mine

⌒

NATURAL WONDERS ABOUND IN and around Ellisville Marsh. *Spartina alterniflora* grows in the low marsh. Piping Plovers nest on the barrier beach. Migratory shorebirds stop over to replenish on their long-haul journeys north and south. There is an astonishing diversity of plant and animal life here. Little do any know that the greatest threat they have ever faced is coming slowly, in the air, in the wind, and in the waves.

Watching a place like Ellisville Marsh on an almost daily basis over fifteen years enables the observer to develop a relationship with nature so intimate that even subtle changes become evident. We become attuned to differences in the water, waves, tides, birds, animals, and plants. Warning signs become apparent.

We pick up the signals as though they have been transmitted to us on a resonant frequency. We can hear through the natural symphony of background noises the crystalized sound of a plover peeping a quarter mile up the beach. We see things in fine detail, and when things fall out of order, or seem different from a day before, a week before, or a year before, we are compelled to look more closely to see if the change is real or imagined. We have witnessed many changes.

Ellisville Marsh is a canary in the coal mine for climate-associated changes occurring along the Atlantic coast. As environmental stewards, we are now witnessing firsthand changes that scientists predicted we would see in the more distant future.

A coastal salt marsh in a place like Ellisville is a gauge for measuring change. And in such sensitive ecosystems, even subtle changes carry consequences.

The ramifications of global climate change are wide ranging, mind blowing: sea level rise, temperature changes in the water and the air, the shifting of the jet stream, more powerful storms, coastal bank erosion, loss of wetlands, degradation of coastal habitat, the breaching of barrier beaches, coastal plain flooding, impacts on groundwater quality, and damage to coastal infrastructure. There are more.

Piping Plovers return to Ellisville Beach from the Bahamas and Florida earlier than in the past. A brief decade ago, the Friends' monitoring team would begin finding the birds in late April, sometimes early May. Now we often see our first plovers by mid-March. Some species no longer leave at all. Great blue herons can be seen wading in the marsh throughout the winter, even when ice has started to form.

The sea level is rising at a rate, scientists estimate, that is faster than any period in the last two thousand years.[1] Although the rising-sea trend may be disguised by daily and seasonal fluctuations, tides are building higher, causing erosion to accelerate along the coastal bank, the cliff edge that borders the sea in places. At Ellisville, Friends volunteers record these changes. The grassy dunes just north of the Ellisville Harbor State Park rock jetty have receded westward by about a hundred feet in the past decade as tides have risen higher.

The exposed coastal bank between Ellisville and Sagamore, a neighbor to the south, is being battered by rising sea level. Increasingly higher tidal surges cause sand to slide down from above. Wind-driven rains from increasingly intense storms pummel the near-vertical surfaces and loosen material up and down the cliff face. Cycles of freezing and thawing contribute to the erosion. Stone revetments do little more than delay the inevitable for property owners whose homes overlooking the sea arc in more precarious positions with each passing year. The beautiful blue-green sea below, which led many to buy their coastal homes in the first place, has become the enemy.

Erosion along the Ellisville Marsh channel has worsened too. The salt marsh fills almost to bursting on some of the highest tides now, especially when there is a strong wind from the east propelling the water in. This causes a higher velocity of flow through the narrow inlet when the tide recedes. Long-established cedar trees on the channel's north side are falling over, their roots undermined by the faster-flowing stream.

Coastal storms are more intense and seem to come with greater frequency. Hurricane-force winds are common during winter nor'easters, driving waves onto the coastline with unaccustomed savagery. Sand is rolled up Ellisville Beach by the storm surge, steepening the slope, which in turn causes more of the water and sand emulsion to slide south.

There is a brownish tinge to the waves hundreds of yards offshore as sand is carried along, even during mild blows. Sand piles up on the north side of rock groins on the beach, creating asymmetric pressure that weakens the structures and dislodges boulders from their decades-long positions in the barriers.

Warming water may be a boon to swimmers in Cape Cod Bay, but it is a bane for some marine mammals, fish, and other sea life. Over the last two decades, ocean temperatures in the northeastern United States have warmed faster than the global ocean average. In fact, the Gulf of Maine, in which Cape Cod Bay sits, has warmed faster than 99 percent of the global ocean.[2]

Ocean warming affects salinity and threatens fish and shellfish populations. Scientific studies suggest that lobsters do not reproduce as well in warmer waters. This has already jeopardized the lobster industry south of Cape Cod.[3] Changing environmental conditions also open the door for an invasion of southern ocean species that have no natural predators in the bay.

Scouring of the intertidal zone, the area that is neither land nor sea, is very much in evidence these days. The rusted metal swing-keel that appears and disappears just off Ellisville Beach is telling. It doesn't move. What moves is everything around it and above it. What the reappearance of the keel tells us is that the elevation of the intertidal zone has been lowered by as much as four feet as sand and cobble have been scoured away by the tides and sideways currents. The water is now deeper there at low tide.

Much of the sediment that used to rest comfortably in the shadow of the inlet is gone, carried south by the waves, moving in sandbars that are, temporarily at least, an idyllic spot for summer beachgoers. This process appears to be accelerating. Sandbars that form in the intertidal zone used to move slowly and deliberately, as if to decide where it would be best to stop and rest. These days a sandbar can move several hundred yards in a season, sometimes in a single storm.

Toward a Sustainable Solution

A sustainable solution that recognizes the importance of the Ellisville Marsh tidal inlet and addresses the problem of inlet blockage is needed. As such, the journey the Friends of Ellisville Marsh embarked on in 2007 is far from over. The organization's founders envisioned their project as a short-term, stopgap intervention that would buy time for the Commonwealth of Massachusetts to design, engineer, and implement a long-term solution to the problem of blockage of the Ellisville Marsh inlet.

Letters signed by MA secretaries of environmental affairs in 2003 and 2008 indicated that the commonwealth recognized its shared responsibility for developing a long-term, sustainable solution to the Ellisville Marsh inlet blockage problem. However, it took a decade from the time of the 2008 letter for state authorities to take their first tangible step in that direction. Appendix B contains a letter sent in 2018 by the Plymouth Select Board on behalf of the Friends urging that the commonwealth take action. Absent such political pressure, it is possible that no action would have been taken. The government's response has come in fits and starts, and no firm commitment has been made to permanently address the problem.

Can the Friends continue to maintain the inlet on an ongoing basis? Barriers exist to relying on the status quo. Reauthorization of local, state, and federal permits is an expensive and wearying process for a small nonprofit. Some Friends' supporters are tired of contributing after more than fifteen years. And the project's supporters would rather see their money being spent on programs that restores the health of the marsh than on permitting. The fact that twice as much has been spent on permitting than the actual work of maintaining the inlet and monitoring the marsh's health since 2007 is deeply troubling.

Recent investigations into alternatives for keeping the Ellisville Marsh inlet open indicate that periodic maintenance by the Friends is by far the lowest-cost option. Moreover, this path is least disruptive to the environment among the options that have been investigated. In Massachusetts, though, the need for frequent repermitting remains a burdensome challenge.

A process that was hoped to lead to a sustainable solution began in 2017. After much "encouragement" from the ranks of Plymouth residents and elected representatives, the commonwealth funded, through its Coastal Community Resilience Grant Program, a project titled "Evaluating Inlet Stabilization at Ellisville Harbor." This project included investigation of a range of alternatives to address the problem of inlet blockage and evaluation of a recommended long-term option.

During the first phase of the project, the Town of Plymouth acted as the lead entity in considering alternatives for a more sustainable tidal inlet system to service the salt marsh and the marsh estuary. John Ramsey, the coastal engineer who advised Vlad Hruby in 2002–3 and published the scientific paper describing what happened after the 2003 inlet reopening, won the competitive bid to provide technical assistance and support to the project.

Following a successful application by the Town's Department of Marine and Environmental Affairs, led by David Gould, the commonwealth provided the town a grant of $111,000 to fund this technical study of alternatives for the sustainable, long-term maintenance of the Ellisville inlet. Then-president Jack Scambos recognized the importance of the award: "The Friends welcome the Commonwealth's show of support with this grant award. Official recognition of the need to identify and fund a long-term solution to the problem of periodic blockage of the Ellisville inlet is a positive development. We look forward to a productive collaboration with the town, its consultant, and the Commonwealth."[4]

From the Town's perspective, ongoing threats to the Ellisville salt marsh system, as well as to coastal homes south of the marsh, are serious concerns. Long-term coastal erosion and the rise in sea level in the coming decades will continue to exacerbate storm-related damage.

The recommended solution emanating from Phase 1 of the project was to restore the badly damaged rock jetty on Ellisville Harbor State Park just north of the inlet to its original 1960 profile with an enhancement. The western end of the jetty would be raised in height to block sand from coming over during major storms. As has already been noted, these storms trigger formation of a barrier spit that blocks the marsh inlet using sand that has been stockpiled by the jetty. In addition, dunes would be restored on the beach north of the inlet. The analytic findings reinforced thinking of the Friends' board members that the rock jetty contributes in a significant way to inlet blockage.

The Phase 1 report recognized that the Friends would need to continue performing periodic maintenance of the inlet under any of the scenarios considered. A follow-on phase of the project (Phase 2) was undertaken by the commonwealth in late 2019 to:

- Advance the preferred conceptual alternative to the preliminary design stage.

- Identify the permits required to construct the preferred alternative.

- Develop comprehensive cost estimates and time lines for both permitting and construction based on the preliminary design.

The project languished, partly because of the COVID-19 pandemic. In late 2021, however, a detailed plan to implement the recommended Phase 2 design was released for review. Upon its review, the Friends' board concluded that the environmental disruption associated with what was being proposed was so significant and the $6 million upfront price tag so high that the organization could no longer support the project moving forward. This turn of events was greatly disappointing to all involved. It became unclear whether the commonwealth would continue the project.

More environmentally benign, "soft" solutions exist, although not all of them have been widely tested and applied. It is uncertain whether soft solutions will be granted regulatory permits in Massachusetts given that the permitting process tends to view new technologies and innovative approaches with distrust. Ellen Russell leads the Friends' investigation into so-called living shoreline or nature-based alternatives. These are largely nonstructural approaches for controlling coastal erosion that absorb energy from ocean waves while at the same time creating habitat for marine organisms. Strategically placed oyster beds fall under this category of solutions. Other projects rely on the hand planting of native vegetation such as *Spartina alterniflora* or dune grass to catch blowing sand. Realistically, though, regulatory filings, permit amendments, and other administrative hurdles stand in the way of doing so.

Russell's first mention of the Friends' interest in investigating soft solutions at an interagency meeting in 2019 was met with scorn by agency officials in the room. One stated bluntly, "This is not permitted in Massachusetts under existing regulations." Asking "Why not?" in meetings with Massachusetts environmental officials has not proven to be productive.

The public official's comment was another indication that environmentally based public interest groups like the Friends are often put into the same basket as real estate developers or other for-profit commercial enterprises. The state's reactions to creative proposals are, at best, guarded. Another underlying philosophy also comes into view. "Allow nothing to be done" is, the Friends' experience suggests, a wetlands restoration doctrine that can be found within some Massachusetts environmental agencies.

More imaginative approaches have been considered to address the inlet blockage problem as well. Mimicking the hands-on approach employed by past stewards of Ellisville Marsh—farmers and fishermen—the Friends began to develop a rapid-response concept that would mobilize a team to hand-dig a trench when the inlet initially becomes blocked.

In the early stage of barrier spit formation, when the spit is typically only a foot or two at its highest point, it is possible to dig a narrow trench through the spit. The trench becomes a sluice for water leaving the marsh when the tide falls. As has been pointed out, the immense volume of water in the marsh out-flow—an average of more than two thousand gallons per second, sustained over several hours—is the natural equivalent of a fire hose. Enabling this rush of water to find a path, however narrow at first, through the blocking spit is a means of restoring the inlet to its most efficient profile. Natural hydraulics powered by the tidal flows can widen and deepen the channel in a matter of one or two cycles even when only a narrow breach has been opened.

After some consideration of the number of people who would be required for the hand-dug approach, the Friends reached out to the Massachusetts Department of Corrections to inquire whether incarcerated people might be formed into a work detail that could be called out on short notice when inlet blockages first occur. The Friends also considered the possibility that incarcerated people might appreciate the opportunity to get some fresh air in a scenic coastal location. One often sees work details of prison

inmates in bright orange jumpers on Massachusetts highways.
Why not at the Ellisville Marsh inlet?

The Department's response was surprisingly positive.
Planning immediately began for the equipment that would be
needed (rakes, shovels, and hip waders). The Friends were told
that a week or so of lead time would be required for a work detail
to be deployed. However, an official at the MassDEP who had
previously said during an Ellisville site visit that permits were
not required for hand work with shovels changed his mind when
the specific possibility of a prison work detail was floated. He
backtracked and indicated that permit amendments would be
required after all.

Four separate permits are maintained by the Friends for inlet
maintenance. Whenever an application for amendment or reauthorization is made, delays typically ensue and new conditions
surface. Based on the change of heart by the MassDEP official,
the idea was reluctantly shelved.

It seems that simple solutions not requiring sophisticated
modeling, consultants, and heavy equipment are not fully considered by the Massachusetts regulatory regime. Some of these
methods had worked well in the past, long before environmental permitting burgeoned. And the light-handed techniques are
typically of low impact to the environment.

Could hollow plastic Jersey barriers filled with sand be put
into temporary use to angle the outgoing flow of water from the
salt marsh across the barrier spit while it is still relatively low?
Could a high-pressure pump be used as a water jet to blast a
trench through the spit to avoid the need for heavy equipment?
Could a fire department pumper truck be brought to the inlet
so that one of its hoses could be used to gouge a path for the
water to flow out of the inlet? All of these practical alternatives
seem to be worth considering. Yet there appears to be an inherent bias against simple solutions, no matter how effective they
might turn out to be.

Each Possible Solution Has Obstacles

What might a sustainable, long-term fix to the problem of recurring blockage of the Ellisville Marsh inlet look like? Most likely, it will be a hybrid solution that combines reconstruction of the rock jetty, dune restoration, placement of wave energy breakers such as oyster beds, and continued, periodic maintenance of the salt marsh inlet on a less frequent basis. The use of heavy construction equipment might be reduced or eliminated by adopting creative approaches. Yet each of the constituent strategies faces its own set of obstacles.

Rebuilding the rock jetty that has defined the north side of the inlet since 1960 to forestall large flows of sand into the inlet during major storms is now presumably "off the table" as the Friends have withdrawn their support for the commonwealth's project due to its drawbacks and uncertainties.

Living shoreline solutions such as oyster beds face their own hurdles. A permit would be required from the US Army Corps of Engineers. And although precedents exist in Massachusetts for this type of approach, the project sites are different. Wellfleet Harbor, where artificial oyster beds have been placed, is very different from Ellisville Harbor. Bureaucratic resistance to innovative approaches can hinge on these differences.

What about the status quo? Continued maintenance of the inlet to reopen storm-induced blockages would seem to be straightforward after more than a decade of site experience. However, there is a catch-22 to combining periodic inlet maintenance with other long-term solutions being considered. If the rock jetty were to be reconstructed and the rebuilt structure functioned as intended, the length of time between maintenance events would probably be extended. Today's one- or two-year maintenance cycle could become four or five years, a problem for the salt marsh ecosystem given the drastic swings in hydraulics. Under this scenario, the Friends would need to renew permits for three- to five-year periods in which no permit work might actually be performed. As we know, there is considerable cost in permitting and repermitting. One cannot simply let permits lapse and assume they can be reauthorized quickly either.

All we can be certain about is that failure to permanently address the problem of inlet blockage will expose this part of the Massachusetts coastline and the sensitive natural resources in Ellisville Marsh to the ravages of climate-related change. We will suffer alongside nature as the economic consequences of our complacency become ever more real. Homes on the coast and in low-lying areas will be structurally compromised. Jobs will be lost in the fishing industry. Our relationship with the natural environment around us will become adversarial. Ellen Russell describes some of the likely consequences:

- Increased erosion of marsh, harbor channel edges, and creek banks due to increased sea level and higher associated tides.

- Increased inundation periods will cause plant root rot and loss of marsh grasses.

- Increased inundation will keep methane gas (CH_4) emissions more "contained" as long as salinities remain above 18 parts per thousand. Methane is a powerful greenhouse gas.

- Increased frequency and intensity of storms are likely to result in increased frequency of inlet reopening work.

- Increased erosion of beach front and coastal bank/ cliff.

- Intrusion of saltwater beneath the shallow freshwater aquifer that may affect drinking water quality for those on private wells.

- Undermining of culvert systems beneath Ellisville Road and Salt Marsh Lane during longer periods of tidal flooding.

- Warming of Cape Cod Bay temperatures, attracting new and different marine species to visit or stay. Losses of species that can't tolerate warmer temperatures.

- Increasing ocean acidification to the point where marine mollusks and crustaceans have difficulty forming calcium carbonate shell.[5]

We are already witnessing the effects of global warming—more powerful storms, coastal erosion, altered migrations of shorebirds, loss of habitat and critical food supplies for both shore and marine species, and declining water quality. According to Dr. Anne Giblin, senior scientist at the Marine Biological Laboratory at Woods Hole, "Historic data would suggest that marshes can't withstand a sea-level rise rate of more than about a centimeter a year." She adds, "There's a real concern that climate change is going to cause us to lose our marshes just at a period of time when there's increased emphasis on their role for storm protection."[6]

What Has Been Learned

The Ellisville Marsh Revitalization Project has opened a window into nature for those who have become involved and committed their energy to solving an environmental problem. It has demonstrated that small environmental rescue projects can be meaningful. They change attitudes and expectations, alter ways of thinking. Deliberate reconnection with nature is a catalyst for developing all sorts of new ideas, along with a fresh perspective. Ripples emanating from the Friends' project have been felt by a widening community of people. Places like Ellisville Marsh awaken the senses and spur us to take climate action on the local level. *All of us.*

Many benefits have been realized by the Friends' project, and its community of supporters feels great pride at having accomplished something meaningful. However, the vision the organization's founders adopted in 2007 remains unrealized. What has been undertaken and accomplished thus far is a remarkable demonstration of the love members of a community can express for their natural surroundings. Such a project should be celebrated not just for the resilience and perseverance its proponents have shown but also for the progress that has been made toward restoring the broken bonds of small, still-wild places with the larger, natural environment from which they have been cut off. In reconnecting with nature, we also reconnect with one another. When we pursue work like this, we learn to feel the pulse of nature beating within us.

The project to revitalize Ellisville Marsh is a gift from a close-knit community to the next generation and to nature. It began as a small statement, grew into a rallying cry, and became a chorus of voices calling for change. No matter its ultimate outcome, this project is a testament to our deep responsibility to live in harmony with our natural surroundings. Even if the project fails to achieve its ultimate objectives, it has already succeeded. It has changed hearts and minds.

All of us have come to feel the pain that Al Marsh felt when the place he knew so intimately was neglected and abused. Through this small and intense project, we all became Al Marsh.

> Albert Boardman Marsh, age 92, of Sagamore Beach, formerly of Plymouth, passed away September 5th at his home surrounded by family.
>
> Al grew up in the Ellisville Village of South Plymouth. While attending Plymouth Schools, he began lobster fishing out of Ellisville Harbor. After graduating, he attended Worcester Polytechnic Institute for two years under a Navy program. Following that, he trained in Pensacola, FL, to become a Navy anti-submarine pilot. He went on to be stationed at Quonset Point, RI, and flew aboard small aircraft carriers. Al later spent two years instructing first year Navy pilots at Whiting Field Naval Base in Milton, FL. He resigned his regular commission in 1956 to return home to Ellisville to raise his family and follow in the

footsteps of his father and grandfather as a commercial fisherman. The remainder of his twenty two year Naval career was with the Reserves at the South Weymouth Naval Air Station, where he became Commanding Officer of his Squadron, retiring in 1971 with the rank of Captain.

Al's career as a commercial lobster fisherman spanned more than forty years. Following retirement, he enjoyed volunteering for many years at the Jordan/BID Hospital in Plymouth. He was an active member of the Swift Memorial United Methodist Church in Sagamore Beach for many years until his passing.

Albert was loved and respected by many. His presence and vibrant spirit will be greatly missed.[7]

The Friends of Ellisville Marsh owe a special debt of gratitude to Al and his family, who gifted much of the Ellisville Marsh property to the Wildlands Trust in 2003. Beyond this, however, Al represented one of our last, and most enduring, connections to this special place. We will always associate his name with the work our organization does at Ellisville Marsh, with heartfelt appreciation.[8]

Conclusion

$\smile$

THIS BOOK IS NOT meant to be political. It espouses neither right- nor left-leaning positions. The views contained in it cannot be characterized as Republican or Democratic. However, a central theme emanating from the Friends' experience is that government policies and behavior must be effective and well timed for the public interest to be served. In the Friends' case, they have not been.

Regulatory permitting has been a millstone around the neck of the Friends of Ellisville Marsh for more than a decade, consuming the energy and enthusiasm of a band of environmental crusaders and diverting their attention from direct, environmental work. Gaining the necessary authorizations to reopen and maintain the Ellisville Marsh inlet has been arduous and costly. A small and thinly funded nonprofit like the Friends, it turns out, is no match for a phalanx of well-funded public agencies that control the environmental permitting process and dictate the outcomes.

The experience has revealed important lessons for regulatory policymakers and agency heads. It is doubtful that Massachusetts is unique in this respect. These lessons are likely to be applicable across a wide variety of environmental permitting projects and many regulatory jurisdictions.

Here are five recommendations for more enlightened thinking about environmental permitting in Massachusetts and beyond. These suggestions do not comprise a proposal for regulatory overhaul. None of these ideas involves loosening regulations or affording a particular kind of applicant special treatment. If implemented sensibly, however, the suggested changes could improve the quality and timeliness of the permitting process and provide badly needed encouragement to environmental restoration and stewardship projects undertaken altruistically and solely in the public interest.

1. Site familiarity—People who work for local, state, and federal agencies that regulate environmental projects, and the people in sister agencies who advise them, should be required to make a site visit before acting. Had this been the case, the Friends likely would not have been compelled to bring in a backhoe to dig up sand and send it to a lab to determine if it was compatible with what makes up the beach 100 yards away.

2. Unified permitting—When an application is received by a permitting agency, the first step should be to rationalize a streamlined roadmap for project permitting. Local, state, and federal agencies should, where possible, follow a unified, interagency permitting process rather than sequential permitting by each respective agency. A small maintenance project involving a salt marsh inlet whose site work typically costs about $5,000 every year or two should not have to spend $64,000 to acquire its initial permits. Nor should the permitting process take two years to complete.

3. Maximizing public benefits—Projects undertaken for the sole purpose of producing environmental benefits, such as enhancement of fisheries and wildlife, tend to be treated by some public agencies in much the same manner as commercial projects that might produce unwanted environmental impacts or collateral damage. A nonprofit whose intent is to revitalize a damaged salt marsh should not be treated in the same way as a commercial property developer.

4. Permit term—The nature of a project and its duration should matter. A project that is understood by all parties to be ongoing and long-term should be eligible for permits that reflect this, especially where historical precedents exist. It makes little sense to require a permit holder to return every three to five years for permit reauthorization when the project is unending. Issuing a permit with a longer term does not lessen public authority over a project. Every agency has a way to revoke its permit if a project is seen to be taking a wrong turn.

5. Data gathering—Data collection and reporting requirements should be subject to a "used and useful" test. When fifteen people from a half-dozen Massachusetts state agencies assemble to decide what conditions should be imposed on a project, they should be required to weigh the importance and usefulness of information to be collected. The Friends' experience suggests that minimal use has been made of the massive trove of environmental monitoring data that has been submitted to public agencies over the past decade. Ironically, the information resource provided by the Friends that appears to have been used most often—high-resolution aerial imagery—was not required under any of the permits.

Several senior officials within Massachusetts environmental agencies were afforded an early view into these recommendations prior to this book manuscript being finalized for publication. Subsequent discussions between these officials and the author highlighted areas of common interest toward improving the regulatory process and enhancing the prospects for success in ecological restoration across the commonwealth.

The author acknowledges that regulatory requirements and processes currently in place have been carefully engineered and are implemented by public officials who take their responsibilities with great seriousness and dedication. The challenge is to make and apply rules in ways that cover the wide diversity of permitting projects that come before these agencies and enable discretion in cases where a clear public benefit has been demonstrated. The Friends are committed to working with the commonwealth toward these ends.

What might the future look like for the Ellisville Marsh Revitalization Project under a more enlightened regulatory regime? Soft solutions such as those considered "living shoreline" might be implemented. Low-tech solutions rooted in historical memory and borne out by decades of experience might be pursued. When a major storm blocks the Ellisville Marsh inlet, a work team might be called out to hand-dig a trench through the newly formed barrier spit so that natural forces, not heavy equipment, could perform the lion's share of the work in restoring the channel to its most hydraulically efficient profile. The multimillion-dollar reconstruction of a hardened coastal structure might become unnecessary.

In a more enlightened world, permits might not be required at all. The resources of nonprofits such as the Friends of Ellisville Marsh could then be redirected from covering endless permitting and repermitting expenses to programs that directly influence recovery of the salt marsh ecosystem to its former, healthier condition. The arduous journey five neighbors set out on in 2007 might finally enter a more satisfying phase, perhaps enabling us to "breathe" more easily. Perhaps the Friends' crusade might actually succeed.

Appendix A

"Ellisville History," by Albert Marsh (1928–2020)

MY GRANDFATHER, OSCAR MARSH, came to Ellisville and lived on the beach as a young man. He met my grandmother, Nancy, they married, and he came to live where we live at the present. He was a lobster fisherman setting approximately seventy traps. The boat he used was a dory propelled by oars and probably had a sail. The boat was very similar to the dories used in the Grand Banks cod fishery. His catches were as high as 300 lobsters a trip. The traps were tended daily weather permitting.

My father, Percy, was born in 1888 and died in 1966. He was born at home, went to school at the Ellisville School and I believe he went to a business school in Lynn. He probably helped with the subsistence farming at home, but his main interest was fishing. He did line trawling for cod, and built a boat here at Ellisville suitable to drag nets for ground fish, that is flounder, cod, and possibly some other species. His main source of income in my lifetime was lobsters.

One of his first boats was a Kingston style lobster boat. He was the first local fisherman to install a gasoline engine. All the other fishermen thought he was "crazy." Later, he had a 28-foot boat built at Clark's harbor in SW Nova Scotia. This boat was quite narrow, probably 8 or 9 feet wide. The engine was a 4-cylinder Palmer. It had two cylinder heads with petcocks to open in order to prime the engine: I don't believe it had a fuel pump. Later he had a 28-foot boat built in East Boston. This had a 10-foot beam, which obviously was much more stable and had more room. It had a 6-cylinder Chrysler Crown.

In the earlier years of my father's lobstering, before my recollection, he sold lobsters to a smack. That is a vessel of some size that may have come from Boston and bought lobsters from various fishermen as it proceeded along the coast. Later he sold to various buyers in Plymouth and on the Cape, sometimes delivering them himself, but mostly storing them in "lobster carrs" until he had enough for a buyer to come with a truck to pick them up.

The "lobster carr" was made of rough spruce lumber. They were 12 feet x 4 feet x 18 inches deep divided into three compartments to separate different size lobsters. The early method of mooring was to select a flat stone, perhaps 3-foot in diameter on the beach below the high tide level. We drilled a hole with a stone drill and sledge. I have helped with this—great fun! A blacksmith would fashion an eye of 1 inch iron bar with a stem long enough to go through the hole and be bent over. About 20 feet of chain would have had an end link enclosed in the eye by the blacksmith—no swivels which were not trusted. The other end of the chain would have a 4-inch diameter ring with a large u-shaped hasp that could be bolted to one end of a mooring pole. This hasp was made of heavy iron stock by the blacksmith. The mooring pole was usually white cedar about 8 feet long by 10 inches in diameter. The top end of the pole had a 1-inch diameter hole drilled through and an oak pin was fashioned to go through the hole and extend 6–8 inches from each end of the hole. A ¾ inch line would have an eye spliced to swivel below the oak pin, the end being fastened to the lobster carr. This same system was used to moor the lobster boats in good weather. They would be moored about 300 yards from the beach.

There were two methods of selling the lobsters. A dip net could be used at the carr, bailing the lobsters into boxes, covering full boxes with burlap and bringing them ashore to be taken to market by truck. The other method was to call the buyer a day ahead, and on the day of sale, tow the carr in about an hour before high tide, pull the carr out of the water, and unload into boxes and into the buyer's truck. The price had been set the day before and they were weighed before loading the truck. This system worked very well. My father was the first to sell to the Snow Inn at Harwichport, but we all sold to them for many years. They treated us very well. When my father was young he sold to a smack which was a coastwise (sailing?) vessel that loaded the lobsters at the mooring. During the Great Depression, the market for lobsters was almost nonexistent. My father at one time had two full carrs and finally sold the entire amount for a nickel apiece regardless of size!

In the warmer months of the year we moored our boats using the same method as lobster carrs. We were only able to enter or leave the harbor about two hours either side of high tide. We very seldom left our boats on the moorings after Nov. 1 so quite often we would put the boats on the mooring in the middle of the night if the weather was favorable—not an easy way to work, but some nights were very beautiful.

My father used a 14-foot dory to get to and from his boat, always using oars. I saw him row ashore when it was blowing pretty stiff southwest—a rugged man! We younger fishermen had square-stern skiffs with 5 or 6 hp outboards to get to our boats. My father always had an open boat with no cabin or shelter. He called the shelters and small cabins we younger men had "ice cream stands"! We all fished in almost any weather. I have been asked if I miss the fishing, and my stock answer is "like a hole in my head," although I do miss it some. We started lobstering about April 1 and finished for the season in mid-December.

All through my grandfather's, father's and earlier years of my lobstering, the lobster "pots" or traps were made from wood, mostly oak, and twine for the entrances. The wood was subject to attack from teredos, a marine worm. My father dipped his pots in a hot barrel of tar. This was done at the beach where he had a large tank with a crude fireplace under it and a drain board beside it to hold the traps after they had been dipped. At that time all the rope was also dipped as it was made from manila or sisal fiber. This did help preserve the fishing gear but was a thoroughly messy job. We younger fishermen gave that process up. The buoys were also wood, becoming somewhat waterlogged part way through the season and had to be changed for lighter ones. Plastic buoys came into use probably in the 60's and vinyl coated wire came into use to build the traps in the 70's. All pots were buoyed individually until the 70's when they began to be set in trawls. The trawls consisted of a ground line that several pots could be fastened to and end lines with buoys. Two men could haul traps much faster than the old system of single pots. Fishermen set many more traps but this put great pressure on the resource. Pots were baited with any fish refuse or bait fish that could be obtained. My father caught some of his bait "cunner," or saltwater perch, in traps especially designed for that purpose. He also speared some in shallow water, mostly sculpins and skates. Fish racks were delivered from New Bedford by truck at one time and redfish from Gloucester.

In the spring, alewife herring were used extensively. In later years sea herring could be bought at the freezer in Sandwich. In earlier years the bait was salted in barrels and stored in fish houses at the beach. Needless to say, in hot weather the bait took on a pretty healthy odor! In the 60's we installed walk-in refrigerated coolers which meant we could keep bait in much better condition. Contrary to some old wives tales, smelly, old bait is not better to use.

Our method of mooring when our boats were in the harbor required fairly extensive work at low tide. We moored on the north side of the channel. We dug holes for four oak poles, placing two poles about ten feet ahead and astern of the site, and two more spaced about one third and alongside from where each end of the boat would be. When digging the holes after we had reached a foot or so below the ground, we would place a barrel with both ends removed to prevent most of the water from entering the hole. We worked the barrel down so that it was mostly below ground. We continued to remove as much gravel inside the barrel as possible. Then the oak poles were lowered into the hole and worked down as far as possible. The poles had been sharpened at the lower end with an axe to provide a chisel point. Two lines had been attached half way up the pole and two men could work the pole down by working the pole back and forth. After the pole had been worked as far down as possible, the remaining space inside the barrel and around it were filed with stones and some gravel. "Dead men" or eight feet or so logs were buried about thirty feet abeam. Lines had been attached to the center of the logs and extended to the breast poles. When the boats were tied up, the lines held the boat upright as the boats were mostly out of water at low tide. Of course there were two other lines, one from the bow pole and one from the stern. Once tied up inside the harbor the boats were in a very safe location until colder weather came and ice formed in the harbor. We tried to have the boats out of the water by mid-December.

THE BREAKWATERS AND CHANNEL: The first breakwater, as far as I know, was constructed of logs forming squares about eight feet on a side. The squares were filled with rocks and arranged in a continuous line, perpendicular to the beach. In the late 1930's arrangements were made with a contractor to build a more substantial jetty and to dredge the channel. Over subsequent years the jetty caught sand coming from the northeast in storms, and the sand and pebbles finally flowed over the jetty into the channel. In 1960 a much more substantial jetty was built and a fairly wide and deep channel was dredged. The depth of the channel never extended below normal low tide, but it did provide enough depth to allow 36-foot boats with 3-foot draft to come and go at half tide. The channel remained good for about ten years although storms eventually filled and buried the north side of the jetty, eventually allowing storms to fill the channel again. Local contractors were hired by the town, and private money was used to clear the channel cach spring and as necessary. This was continued until

1987 when the Commonwealth stopped any further work until environmental permits and engineering plans were provided.

Two of the older fishermen nearing retirement and I moved to the Sandwich Marina harbor at the east end of the Canal. Major northeast storms in the next few years made the Ellisville channel mostly unusable. Tremendous amounts of gravel flowed in a southerly direction, changing the beach south of the beach opening a great deal. The beach changed in each storm and eventually caused extreme erosion to Dr. Hruby's property. He acquired permits and plans to reopen the channel as it had been in 1986 or so. This was accomplished in about 2004.

SEA MOSSING: In the early 1940's we started harvesting Irish sea moss. This was accomplished by starting an hour or so before low tide and continuing the same time after low tide. We would each have our dory or skiff, and usually filled them to capacity. We used a specially constructed rake with long (6 +/- inch) curved teeth and a handle about 6-inch diameter and 16 feet long. We always enjoyed this work—unless the wind came up! The moss would make your hands as white as snow. When the tide came in, we brought the loaded boats into the harbor and spread the moss on the beach to dry. We would turn it a time or two, and after a day or two, pack the moss in burlap bags and bring to the barn until we had enough to call for a truck to take it to a buyer that was in Scituate??? Later in the 1950's the moss was sold wet each day and taken to a buyer in Kingston where it was dried in a machine similar to a clothes dryer except much larger. This relieved the individual "mosser" from a great deal of work. There were times when we could harvest moss twice a day when the low tides came at each end of the daytime-HARD WORK! But we enjoyed it.

COD FISHING: In the early 1960's we learned about a system of catching cod on hand lines which was new to us. The line was 300 lb test monofilament with a stainless Norwegian jig at the end. About two feet above the jig we fastened a single hook imbedded in a rubber "worm." The most common size jig weighed

27 oz, but we had other sizes from 17 oz to 42 oz. The various sizes were used in order to get the jig to the bottom depending on wind and drift speed. Two or more worms could be fastened at intervals above that. We fished mostly on ledges about three miles or so from the beach. The cod seemed to come into the bay in the late fall to spawn. We caught many large females which had scratches on their underbelly indicating they had scraped or forced the spawn from their bodies by scraping against the rocky bottom. We never anchored, but found the fish in fairly small spots from one year to the next.

In December 1962 my father and I caught just under 1,700 pounds dressed weight of cod in one afternoon and the next morning. The fish were mostly large weighing as much as 70 pounds. We sold them at Sandwich and Plymouth and then they were shipped to New York. In subsequent years the catch fell off until it became almost non-existent.

   —*"Ellisville History" has been included with the permission of the Estate of Albert B. Marsh.*

Appendix B

Facsimile of Letter from Plymouth Select Board to Massachusetts
Secretary of Energy and Environmental Affairs, May 15, 2018

TOWN OF PLYMOUTH
26 Court Street
Plymouth, Massachusetts 02360
(508) 747-1620

The Honorable Matthew Beaton
Secretary of Energy and Environmental Affairs
Commonwealth of Massachusetts
100 Cambridge Street, Suite 900
Boston, MA 02114
May 15, 2018

Dear Secretary Beaton:

Re: Working Together to Create a Long-term Solution to the Problem of Blockage of the Ellisville Marsh Inlet (Project reference: Chapter 91 Waterways Permit No. 12735; 401 Water Quality Certification No. X228224)

The Town of Plymouth has a strong interest in working with the Executive Office of Energy and Environmental Affairs to implement a permanent solution to the longstanding problem of blockage of the Ellisville Marsh inlet. A local nonprofit (Friends of Ellisville Marsh, Inc.-FoEM) that has been maintaining this inlet for most of the past decade recently made the Town aware of challenges associated with their ability to continue doing so. We believe it is imperative that we act together now to improve the odds of long-term project success. This letter provides background to the problem and a description of the current situation. *Specifically, we ask that you exercise your leadership to spur all stakeholders into action to build a sustainable and permanent solution to this problem. A solid foundation of environmental data and project experience already exists and collaboration between your departments, the Town, and FoEM will insure a much needed, long-term outcome.*

BACKGROUND AND DESCRIPTION OF THE PROBLEM

71-acre Ellisville Marsh is one of Plymouth's most prized natural resources. It is designated as both an Area of Critical Environmental Concern (ACEC)[1] and a Massachusetts Important Bird Area (IBA). Very few sites statewide are so recognized. However, for over a century the inlet to Ellisville Marsh has been subject to periodic blockages caused by avulsion when winter storms hit the Massachusetts coast. During these events, massive volumes of sand are washed into the inlet channel, exceeding the capability of the channel's natural hydraulics to clear it out. A barrier spit instantly forms, diverting the inlet southward and, once the spit has grown to a certain length over a period of weeks or months, introduces resistance to tidal flows. Tidal exchange inside the marsh is impacted and native plants such as *Spartina alterniflora* and *Spartina patens,* as well as fisheries and wildlife, suffer. Approximately half of the marsh itself falls within Ellisville Harbor State Park and all of it lies within the Ellisville Harbor ACEC so the ecological cost of environmental degradation at this site is very high.

For much of the twentieth century, local fishermen operating out of Ellisville Harbor routinely maintained the inlet; however, this practice was forcibly halted by the Commonwealth in 1987. Notwithstanding this action, historical records indicate that state agencies have long recognized the blockage problem, performing work on the Ellisville Marsh inlet and preparing related engineering plans several times in the past (1917, 1939, 1951 and 1960). Moreover, two recent Secretaries of Environmental Affairs have stated that the Commonwealth shares responsibility for developing a long-term solution to the problem (see attached MEPA certificates—2003 and 2008).

RECENT EVENTS

Since 2007, a local 501(c)(3) nonprofit organization known as the Friends of Ellisville Marsh (FoEM) has raised funds, obtained all the necessary local, state and federal regulatory permits and performed periodic maintenance of the Ellisville inlet. The cost to FoEM of obtaining all necessary regulatory permits was $64,000 and actual maintenance work over the past eight years has cost a total of $28,000. The disturbing imbalance between the necessary regulatory expense and the cost of actual work for this small, but important, project is something that should be addressed. FoEM has done this without the help of taxpayer funds or paid staff. They have bought time for a long-term solution to be identified, engineered and implemented. Indeed, their organization has always viewed their interventions as a necessary, stopgap measure until a permanent solution could be found. FoEM has expressed concern to the Town that its current Chapter 91 waterways permit is set to expire in July of next year and that it will be very difficult for them to justify another large expense to obtain the replacement permit, especially when site conditions are largely the same as they were when the initial permit was issued in 2010. Consistent with this, renewal of the existing permit should be routine and *pro forma*.

In 2017, the Town of Plymouth completed a key project, "Evaluating Inlet Stabilization at Ellisville Harbor," funded largely by a grant under MA CZM's Coastal Community Resilience Grant Program. This feasibility study for pre-design alternatives included participation by the Town of Plymouth, FoEM, and staff from CZM, DCR, NHESP and the MassDEP and produced a set of recommendations designed to make the inlet more stable and tidal flows more consistent. Virtually all of the recommended work would take place on the north side of the inlet, inside Ellisville Harbor State Park, rather than on Shifting Lots Preserve, the Wildlands Trust property on the inlet's south side where FoEM operates. As the property owner DCR will need to be the permit applicant.

The punishing winter of 2017–18 made the urgency of work toward a long-term solution at the Ellisville Marsh inlet even more compelling. Five major storms hit the Massachusetts coastline, each of which struck a blow to the Ellisville Marsh inlet. Because several storms occurred in late March and early April, FoEM was unable to schedule inlet maintenance and, as a result, the degree of tidal flow restriction is at its worst in the last ten years.

CURRENT CONDITIONS

The Ellisville Marsh inlet is currently blocked by a barrier spit of approximately 1,000 feet in length, sufficiently long to negatively impact the marsh ecosystem based on the findings of past scientific studies. Moreover, there is now what amounts to a "hairpin turn" in the inlet channel where the diversion begins and this slows the flow velocity to virtually zero, compounding the effect of the lengthened channel path. Water is backed up in the marsh and the tidal range is directly affected, a fact which is likely to be confirmed scientifically by FoEM's tidal pressure gauges this summer. Erosion of the channel bank on the north side (Ellisville Harbor State Park) accelerated due to the recent succession of major storms, as well as scouring associated with the sharp turn in the channel. Continuing erosion of the dune and deterioration of the rock jetty on the state park side of the inlet have also been fairly dramatic. These impacts are likely to be exacerbated by rising sea levels going forward.

Completion of the study of inlet alternatives last year created an important opportunity to jump-start the kind of public/private partnership suggested by the attached MEPA certificates. The Town of Plymouth and FoEM request that we join forces with the agencies under your leadership to design a permanent solution and implement it in a timely way. It has been fifteen years since the Commonwealth acknowledged its interest in the Ellisville Marsh inlet. The fact that FoEM has successfully addressed the immediate problem does not reduce the need for an ultimate solution. The time for a long-term, sustainable approach is now.

We look forward to discussing with you the best approach to move this project forward.

Sincerely,

Kenneth Tavares, Chairman

c: David Gould
Eric Cody, Friends of Ellisville Marsh, Inc.
Vinny deMacedo, Senator
William Keating, Congressman
Randy Hunt, Representative

Notes

Chapter 1: A Place Called Ellisville Marsh

1. For a description of pine barrens, see "The Massachusetts Coastal Pine Barrens: An Overview," Southeastern Massachusetts Pine Barrens Alliance, https://pinebarrensalliance.org/the-massachusetts-coastal-pine-barrens-an-overview/.
2. Tidmarsh Wildlife Sanctuary, Mass Audubon, https://www.mass audubon.org/get-outdoors/wildlife-sanctuaries/tidmarsh.
3. Living Observatory, https://www.livingobservatory.org/.
4. Gershon Dublon and Joseph A. Paradiso, "How a World Filled with Sensors Will Change the Way We See, Hear, Think and Live," *Scientific American*, July 2014, 36–41.
5. Friends of Ellisville Marsh, Inc., www.ellisvillemarsh.org.
6. *The Journal of Henry D. Thoreau*, ed. Bradford Torrey and Francis H. Allen, vols. 1–7 (New York: Dover, 1962), 1158 (June 15, 1857).
7. Torrey and Allen, 1158.
8. "Ellisville Harbor, Plymouth," unpublished document, MA Department of Conservation and Recreation, received January 12, 2009.
9. Wildlands Trust, https://wildlandstrust.org/.
10. National Oceanic and Atmospheric Administration, "What Is a Salt Marsh?" National Ocean Service, https://oceanservice.noaa.gov/facts/saltmarsh.html.
11. Russell quoted in Eric Cody, letter to the editor, "Why Salt Marshes Are Important," *Old Colony Memorial*, February 1, 2020.
12. Russell quoted in Cody, letter to the editor.
13. The names Ellisville Harbor and Ellisville Marsh are used interchangeably; however, the harbor is located within the marsh.
14. Massachusetts Audubon Society, Massachusetts Important Bird Areas (IBA), https://www.massaudubon.org/our-conservation-work/wildlife-research-conservation/statewide-bird-monitoring/massachusetts-important-bird-areas-iba; eBird, Ellisville Harbor State Park hotspot, https://ebird.org/hotspot/L265654.
15. James Winthrop, "Journal of Survey in 1791, for a Canal Across

Cape Cod," Boston Public Library Historical Manuscripts, Hist. Ref. E173, 74.

16. Edward L. Bell, "Cultural Resources on the New England Coast and Continental Shelf: Research, Regulatory, and Ethical Considerations from a Massachusetts Perspective," *Coastal Management* 37, no. 1 (2009): 17–53.

17. According to botanist Irina Kadis, the plant was most likely sweet pepperbush (*Clethra alnifolia*), more commonly known as "soap bush." According to multiple sources, the leaves of sweet pepperbush contain an antibacterial compound that lathers like soap when one rubs them on the skin with water.

18. The word "Wampanoag" translates literally to "People of the First Light." Alternative names for the tribe found at https://www.her ringpondtribe.org/our-history/.

19. One theory is that the plague was smallpox introduced by European traders and fishermen.

20. A salt pond is a coastal water resource not connected to the sea by a surface channel but whose hydrology and salinity are significantly influenced by the tides.

21. Historical records and interviews with longtime Ellisville residents indicate that all those who fished or engaged in lobstering from Ellisville Harbor were men, hence the use of the male gender in this context. This was not the case for many other New England locations.

22. According to Nancy Marsh Terry, Al Marsh's daughter, two other lobstermen—Bob Glass and George Swift from Cedarville—continued to operate their boats out of Ellisville Harbor until the channel became unnavigable.

Chapter 2: How It Is, How It Was

1. Ellisville Harbor was designated a harbor of safe refuge in 1961. According to the Code of Federal Regulations, "harbor of safe refuge" refers to a port, inlet, or other body of water normally sheltered from heavy seas by land in which a vessel can navigate and safely moor.

2. Betsy Puckett, email to author, January 24, 2018.

3. Ernest Clifton Ellis, "Reminiscences of Ellisville," *Old Colony Memorial*, July 13, 1972, 31.

4. One fish weir continues to operate in Chatham, MA. See Chatham Fish Weirs Enterprises, https://m.facebook.com/Chatham-Fish -Weirs-Enterprises-115932041823146/.

5. Ellis, "Reminiscences of Ellisville," 36.

6. Ellis, 37.

7. This intent is indirectly expressed in the January 16, 1980, letter signed by Massachusetts Secretary of Environmental Affairs John A. Berwick that established the Ellisville Harbor ACEC, https://www .mass.gov/files/documents/2016/08/tu/er-des.pdf.

8. The MA Department of Environmental Management merged with the Metropolitan District Commission in 2003 to become the MA Division of Conservation and Recreation. Commonwealth of Massachusetts, Department of Environmental Management, Wetlands Restriction Order for Ellisville, December 2, 1981, 2–3.
9. Jim Baker, "Sea Moss in Plymouth: Greg White Remembers," unpublished manuscript, 2020, typescript.
10. Jack Scambos, "Ellisville Memories" (unpublished), June 15, 2020.
11. Friends of Ellisville Marsh, *Newsletter*, December 2015, 2, https://secureservercdn.net/72.167.242.48/bn1.5ce.myftpupload.com/wp-content/uploads/2021/08/Friends-of-Ellisville-Marsh-Newsletter_Dec-2015.pdf.

Chapter 3: Plants under Siege

1. See http://www.salicicola.com/checklists/Ellisville/.
2. Irina Kadis, communication with author, April 2021.
3. See the phragmites fact sheet at https://www.ontario.ca/page/phragmites-fact-sheet.
4. Judith Weis/The Conversation, "Climate Change Is Putting This Invasive Species to Good Use," *Popular Science*, April 9, 2019, https://www.popsci.com/phragmites-invasive-climate-change/; Kadis, communication with author.
5. For further details, see MN Department of Agriculture, "Spotted Knapweed," https://www.mda.state.mn.us/plants/pestmanagement/weedcontrol/noxiouslist/spottedknapweed.
6. Joe Alper, "Wicked Weed of the West," *Smithsonian Magazine*, December 2004, https://www.smithsonianmag.com/science-nature/wicked-weed-of-the-west-97008935/.
7. Roundup is a brand-name herbicide that contains the active ingredient glyphosate. Glyphosate is a highly controversial chemical whose use, it has been claimed by some scientists, can cause cancer. A number of countries have either banned its use or are considering such a ban.
8. Kadis, communication with author.
9. Friends of Ellisville Marsh, *Newsletter*, December 2016, 3–4, https://secureservercdn.net/72.167.242.48/bn1.5ce.myftpupload.com/wp-content/uploads/2021/08/Friends-of-Ellisville-Marsh-Newsletter_December-2016.pdf.

Chapter 4: The Crux of the Problem

1. Ernest Clifton Ellis, "Reminiscences of Ellisville," *Old Colony Memorial*, July 13, 1972, 10.
2. "The Portland Gale of 1898, and the Cat that Saved a Life," New England Historical Society, updated 2022, https://www.newenglandhistoricalsociety.com/the-portland-gale-of-1898-and-the-cat-that-saved-a-life/.

3. The Gulf of Maine is the large area bounded on the south by Cape Cod and on the north by Cape Sable Island in Nova Scotia. It includes the coastlines of New Hampshire and Maine, as well as most of the Massachusetts coast. The Chatham bar is a well-known example of how shifting sands dynamically define the Massachusetts coastline.

4. *Annual Highlights of the Friends of Ellisville Marsh 2012–2013*, July 15, 2013, https://secureservercdn.net/72.167.242.48/bn1.5ce.myftpupload.com/wp-content/uploads/2021/08/annual-report-2012-13.pdf.

5. Carolyn Y. Johnson, "Cause Sought as Marshes Turn into Barren Flats," *Boston Globe*, July 17, 2006, http://archive.boston.com/news/local/massachusetts/articles/2006/07/17/cause_sought_as_marshes_turn_into_barren_flats/.

6. Doug Fraser, "Cape's Disappearing Salt Marsh," *Cape Cod Times*, February 18, 2015.

7. Jan P. Smith and Marc Carullo, "Survey of Potential Marsh Dieback Sites in Coastal Massachusetts," prepared for the Massachusetts Bays National Estuary Program and MA Office of Coastal Zone Management, April 2007, https://www.google.com/url?sa=t&rct=j&q=&esrc=s&source=web&cd=&ved=2ahUKEwjkub6uxfj3AhWBk4kEHd-eBiIQFnoECDMQAQ&url=https%3A%2F%2Fwww.mass.gov%2Fdoc%2Fsurvey-of-potential-marsh-dieback-sites-in-coastal-massachusetts%2Fdownload&usg=AOvVaw1oVf_lboyYUSFd8iH_o.

8. William Hubbard, Friends of Ellisville Marsh, "Gem in Our Midst: History and Rescue of Ellisville Marsh," August 27, 2015, 31.

9. Comments submitted to Massachusetts Department of Environmental Protection by Ed Reiner, senior wetland scientist, US Environmental Protection Agency, June 11, 2003, in the case of Vlad Hruby (File no. ACOP-SE-06-6Y003), based on his inspection of Ellisville Marsh on October 2, 2002.

10. Ellen K. Russell, "Factors Influencing *Spartina alterniflora* Productivity in Relationship to Estuary Inlet Reopening, Ellisville Marsh, Plymouth, MA" (PhD diss., University of Massachusetts–Amherst, 2019), https://scholarworks.umass.edu/dissertations_2/1759/.

11. The number of sampling plots for ongoing data collection has since been reduced to around fifty.

12. John S. Ramsey, High E. Ruthven, Sean W. Kelley, and Brian L. Howes, "Quantifying the Influence of Inlet Migration on Tidal Marsh System Health," *Proceedings of the 30th International Conference on Coastal Engineering*, ed. Jane McKee Smith (2006, San Diego, CA), 2082–94, https://www.worldscientific.com/worldscibooks/10.1142/6439.

Chapter 5: Birth of a Backyard Movement

1. In fact, the attachment to the consent order relating to the formation of a nonprofit was drafted by Attorney Quinn and presented to the MassDEP, which adopted his language verbatim in the order.

2. Massachusetts Department of Environmental Protection, Administrative Consent Order with Penalty and Notice of Non-compliance, File no. ACOP-SE-06–6Y003, December 14, 2006, 8.

3. New England Electric System became National Grid USA in 2000.

4. Piping Plovers began returning to crowded urban beaches around Boston in 2007 and have returned to nest there since. See "Piping Plovers Parade Revere Beach, boston.com, http://archive.boston.com/news/local/gallery/plovers_revere_beach/.

5. Friends of Ellisville Marsh, *Newsletter*, Fall 2019, 2–3, https://secure servercdn.net/72.167.242.48/bn1.5ce.myftpupload.com/wp-content/uploads/2021/08/Newsletter_Fall_2019.pdf.

6. Sarah Cowles, email correspondence with author, February 3, 2021.

Chapter 6: A Thousand Paper Cuts

1. Mass Audubon, "Coastal Waterbird Program," https://www.mass audubon.org/our-conservation-work/wildlife-research-conservation/coastal-waterbird-program.

2. The agencies' official names are Massachusetts Department of Conservation and Recreation (DCR), Massachusetts Department of Environmental Protection (MassDEP), Massachusetts Division of Marine Fisheries (MDMF), Natural Heritage and Endangered Species Program (NHESP), and Massachusetts Office of Coastal Zone Management (MCZM).

3. Several hundred thousand dollars have, however, been committed by the commonwealth to studies of how to stabilize the Ellisville inlet over the long term.

4. "North Shore Residents Concerned about Health Impacts of Landfill, Incinerator," Boston 25 News, November 16, 2017, https://www.boston25news.com/news/north-shore-residents-concerned-about-health-impacts-of-landfill-incinerator/648793794/.

5. Ortho photographs are extremely high-resolution images captured from an aircraft. The image is referenced to a set of ground control points that establish vertical elevation relative to a surveyed benchmark such as a National Geodetic Survey medallion. This enables the final product to be converted into a survey map. The Friends used this technology to create its first "existing conditions plan" for permitting purposes.

6. Friends of Ellisville Marsh, *Newsletter*, March 2014, 2, https://secure servercdn.net/72.167.242.48/bn1.5ce.myftpupload.com/wp-content/uploads/2021/08/Friends-of-Ellisville-Marsh-Newsletter_March-2014.pdf.

Chapter 7: Breaching the Spit

1. A time-of-year restriction that begins on April 1 precludes maintenance dredging for the protection of marine fisheries, such as winter

flounder. The restriction also recognizes the start of the nesting season for such threatened shorebirds as Piping Plovers.

2. John S. Ramsey, High E. Ruthven, Sean W. Kelley, and Brian L. Howes, "Quantifying the Influence of Inlet Migration on Tidal Marsh System Health," *Proceedings of the 30th International Conference on Coastal Engineering*, ed. Jane McKee Smith (2006, San Diego, CA), 2092.

3. Friends of Ellisville Marsh, *Newsletter*, Spring 2018, 2, https://secure servercdn.net/72.167.242.48/bn1.5ce.myftpupload.com/wp-content /uploads/2021/08/Newsletter_Spring_2018.pdf.

4. Friends, *Newsletter*, Spring 2018, 1.

Chapter 8: The Closer You Look

1. Specific water quality monitoring requirements have varied over the years.

2. George Japoshvili and Ellen Russell, "A New Parasitization Record of *Haliaspis spartinae* (Diaspididae) and *Encarsia ellisvillensis* sp. nov. (Chalcidoidea: Aphelinidae) from the United States," *Annals of the Entomological Society of America* 105, no. 3 (May 1, 2012), https:// academic.oup.com/aesa/article/105/3/493/15324.

3. Friends of Ellisville Marsh, Special Announcement: New Species of Wasp Found in Ellisville Marsh, November 2010, https://secure servercdn.net/72.167.242.48/bn1.5ce.myftpupload.com/wp-content /uploads/2022/06/new-species_Nov-2010.pdf.

4. Beach transect measurements were required under permits for a number of years, but the requirement was subsequently waived.

5. HOBO data loggers are a product of Onset Computer Corporation, Bourne, MA.

Chapter 9: Invisible Birds

1. The Piping Plover is listed on the federal and Massachusetts endangered species list as a threatened species. Least Terns are listed by Massachusetts as a species of special concern but have been removed from the federal endangered species list.

2. See, for example, "Lawsuit Charges New York Parks with Violating Endangered Species Act," American Bird Conservancy, March 31, 2016, https://abcbirds.org/article/lawsuit-charges-new-york-parks -with-violating-endangered-species-act/.

3. US Fish and Wildlife Service Northeast Region, "Happy Mother's Day!," May 11, 2013. https://usfwsnortheast.wordpress.com/2013/05/11 /happy-mothers-day/photo-by-heidi-sanders-friends-of-ellisville -marsh-inc-plymouth-ma-c2012-courtesy-eric-cody-friends-of-el lisville/.

Chapter 10: Detoxifying a Pond

1. A Massachusetts great pond is defined as any pond or lake that covered more than ten acres in its natural state.
2. *Town of Plymouth Pond and Lake Atlas*, final report, June 2015, https://www.plymouth-ma.gov/natural-resources/files/pondsplymouth pondsandlakesstewardshipatlasjune2015.
3. Savery Pond has also been named in the US Environmental Protection Agency's Massachusetts Section 303(d) List of Impaired Waters.
4. For information on the New England Grassroots Environment Fund, visit https://grassrootsfund.org/.
5. Peter Schwartzman, email exchange with author, April 12, 2021.
6. Peter Schwartzman, communication with author, April 12, 2021.
7. Rob Moir, "Harmful Algae Lurking in Bartlett Pond, Plymouth MA," Ocean River Institute, July 24, 2018, https://www.oceanriver.org/2018/07/24/algae-smothering-bartlett-pond-plymouth-ma/.
8. See https://www.saverypond.org/.

Chapter 11: Natural Wonders

1. New England Aquarium, "Aquarium News and Updates," January 15, 2016, http://news.neaq.org/2016/01/dog-finds-stranded-turtle.html.
2. NOAA Fisheries, Species Directory, "North Atlantic Right Whale," https://www.fisheries.noaa.gov/species/north-atlantic-right-whale.

Chapter 12: Canary in the Coal Mine

1. Erin Blakemore, "Sea Levels Are Rising More Quickly Than in the Last Two Millennia," *Smithsonian Magazine*, February 22, 2016, https://www.smithsonianmag.com/smart-news/sea-levels-are-rising-more-quickly-last-two-millennia-180958200/.
2. NOAA Fisheries Science Center, "Climate Change in the Northeast U.S. Shelf Ecosystem," January 2021, https://www.fisheries.noaa.gov/new-england-mid-atlantic/climate/climate-change-northeast-us-shelf-ecosystem.
3. David Abel, "Losing Hope for Lobster South of Cape Cod," *Boston Globe*, December 2, 2017.
4. Friends of Ellisville Marsh, "Town of Plymouth Wins $111,000 Grant to Evaluate Long-Term Options for the Ellisville Inlet," special announcement, August 2016, https://secureservercdn.net/72.167.242.48/bn1.5ce.myftpupload.com/wp-content/uploads/2022/06/Announcement-August2016.pdf.
5. Friends of Ellisville Marsh, *Newsletter*, October 23, 2019, 1–2, https://secureservercdn.net/72.167.242.48/bn1.5ce.myftpupload.com/wp-content/uploads/2021/08/Newsletter_Fall_2019.pdf.

6. Giblin quoted in Miriam Wasser, "Here's What the New U.N. Report on Oceans and Ice Means for New England," WBUR, September 25, 2019. https://www.wbur.org/news/2019/09/25/ipcc-oceans-ice-massachusetts-northeast-takeaways.

7. Excerpted from Albert Boardman Marsh, 92, obituary, *Cape Cod Times*, posted online on September 09, 2020, https://www.capecod times.com/obituaries/story-obituaries-2020-09-09-albert-boardman-marsh-92-114054054.

8. Friends of Ellisville Marsh, *Newsletter*, "End of an Era: Albert Marsh, 1928–2020," https://secureservercdn.net/72.167.242.48/bn1.5ce.myft pupload.com/wp-content/uploads/2021/08/Newsletter-Fall-2020_compressed.pdf.

Appendix B: Facsimile of Letter from Plymouth Select Board to Massachusetts Secretary of Energy and Environmental Affairs, May 15, 2018

1. It is noteworthy that the mouth of the inlet at Cape Cod Bay is shown on ACEC maps as a "carve-out," enabling the historical practice of inlet maintenance to continue after the ACEC was created.

Index

ERIC P. CODY is cofounder and president of the Friends of Ellisville Marsh, Inc., a 501(c)(3) environmental nonprofit in Plymouth, Massachusetts. He has, since 2007, committed thousands of hours to the organization's efforts to revitalize Ellisville Marsh, the town's environmental gem. As a former energy industry executive and consultant, Cody has written extensively about complex energy systems and energy markets in numerous articles, reports, white papers, and case studies in print and online over a period of forty years. This is the first time he has written about a complex environmental system. He holds a Bachelor of Arts degree from Amherst College and a Master in City and Regional Planning degree from Harvard University. He and his wife, Christine, are both former Naval officers. They live on a bluff overlooking Cape Cod Bay in Ellisville, Massachusetts.